The Pond Doctor

Planning & Maintaining a Healthy Water Garden

Helen Nash

With Photographs by Ronald E. Everhart

Sterling Publishing Co., Inc. New York

cover photo:
Nymphaea 'Peace,' a new hybrid from Bee Fork Water Gardens, Brentwood, Missouri.
Photo by Michael F. Duff.

title page photo:
N. 'Atropurpurea'

page four photo:
N. Arc-en-Ciel, although beautiful, is grown primarily for its foliage.

Designed by Judy Morgan

Library of Congress Cataloging-in-Publication Data

Nash, Helen, 1944–
    The pond doctor : planning & maintaining a healthy water garden   /
Helen Nash ; illustrated by Ronald E. Everhart.
        p.   cm.
    Includes index.
    ISBN 0-8069-0686-3
    1. Water gardens.   2. Water garden pests—Control.   I. Title.
SB423.N37   1994
635.9'674—dc20   94-19956
                                  CIP

635.9
NAS

1 3 5 7 9 10 8 6 4 2

Published by Sterling Publishing Company, Inc.
387 Park Avenue South, New York, N.Y. 10016
© 1994 by Helen Nash
Distributed in Canada by Sterling Publishing
℅ Canadian Manda Group, P.O. Box 920, Station U
Toronto, Ontario, Canada M8Z 5P9
Distributed in Great Britain and Europe by Cassell PLC
Villiers House, 41/47 Strand, London WC2N 5JE, England
Distributed in Australia by Capricorn Link (Australia) Pty Ltd.
P.O. Box 6651, Baulkham Hills, Business Centre, NSW 2153, Australia
Printed and Bound in Hong Kong
All rights reserved

Sterling ISBN 0-8069-0686-3

With great affection and appreciation to John and Mary Mirgon, who have so generously shared their time, knowledge, and love of the water lily with so many around the world.

Tropical water lily, 'John Mirgon,' hybridized
by Charles Winch of Sydney, Australia.
Photographed by John Mirgon.

With warmth and appreciation to Michael Duff, the consummate hobbyist and transplanted New Zealander, whose love of the water lily knows no geographical bounds.

Hardy water lily, 'James Brydon,' hybridized
by Dreer in 1900. Photographed by
Michael F. Duff.

And to my husband, Dave, whose devotion and support brought water lilies into my life and made this work possible.

CONTENTS

INTRODUCTION

Moistened stone, trickling water,
Shimmering fish—
And the lily opens.
— Helen Nash

The Pond Doctor is the result of my own personal odyssey into water gardening. What began as a simple, commercial venture of growing water lilies became an at times frustrating, hands-on learning experience. Mistakes were made. Disasters occurred. I monopolized the information desk at the Indianapolis Public Library as I played Sherlock Holmes, tracking down people and companies involved in but the slightest way in any aspect of water gardening. My telephone bills assumed monstrous proportions as I called around the world asking questions, verifying information, or simply corroborating information. I became obsessed with the purchase of new and unique stamps with which to grace my correspondence.

Although my odyssey continues, I have learned a few basic things: It usually takes less effort to prevent a problem than it does to solve it. Available resources or a single source may not contain the full scope of repercussions created by pond conditions. Since our modern age is full of daily discoveries, there may be no one correct way of handling a pond situation. Because even experts and authorities may disagree on information, it is always wise to seek corroboration. And while the sharing of hands-on experience may not be scientifically valid, it is an invaluable source of information in the practical ownership of a pond.

In *The Pond Doctor* I have tried to create a practical and usable resource of problem prevention and rem-

N. 'Angélique,' a new hybrid from Bee Fork Nurseries, in Missouri. Photographed by Michael F. Duff.

edies. Although scientific research and corroboration played a part in understanding remedies, the book itself is not intended as a scientific treatise or authority. Nor is it meant to offer the only solutions to problems. It is intended merely to answer some questions and to offer some solutions to help make pond-ownership the experience we desire—aesthetically pleasing, spiritually soothing, and wondrously fascinating.

Helen Nash
January 1994

chapter one

POND SITING

*Less-than-ideal sites can be transformed to
accommodate a pond.*

ROOT INVASION

Tree roots will extend underground as far as the branches extend aboveground. Vigorous trees, such as willows, may quickly invade the pool area. It may be necessary to regularly trench and sever the invading roots. However, extensive cutting of the roots may damage or kill the offending tree. Invasive trees may

***B**esides limiting plant selections to shade-tolerant varieties, siting a pond near trees may require a fiberglass lining to prevent root intrusions.*

have to be removed altogether. Transplant them during winter dormancy, if possible. If a tree cannot be removed, the pool may have to be rebuilt elsewhere or as an aboveground structure.

Some grasses and weeds, such as nutgrass, may rupture concrete or penetrate the thickest of liners. Keep them pulled or treat carefully with a systemic herbicide, taking care to avoid spraying the chemical into the pool water or where it might be washed into the pond. In the case of a liner-constructed pool, it may be necessary to dismantle the pool and install fiberglass underlay to prevent most roots from penetration.

RUN-OFF CONTAMINATION

Setting the pool edging at an angle down and away from the pond will prevent light run-offs from entering the water. The slight elevation of the pool edge can be camouflaged by plants and rocks. A retaining wall can also be constructed on the high-ground side of the pond. The wall should extend out beyond the width of

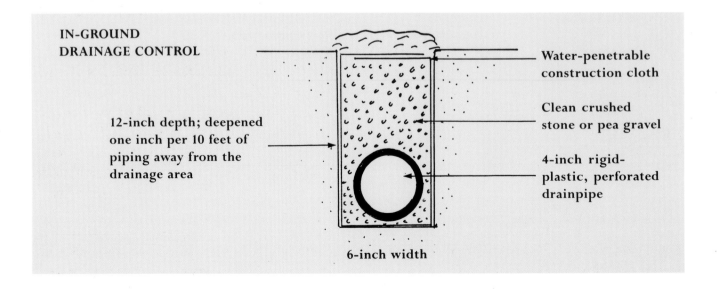

IN-GROUND DRAINAGE CONTROL

12-inch depth; deepened one inch per 10 feet of piping away from the drainage area

Water-penetrable construction cloth

Clean crushed stone or pea gravel

4-inch rigid-plastic, perforated drainpipe

6-inch width

the pool. Effective for diverting light to normal run-offs, the wall may actually function as a waterfall in the event of heavy run-offs.

An effective solution is to dig a 12-inch-deep trench 6 inches wide between the run-off source and the pool. The trench should be deepened by one inch per ten feet of length. The open end of the drainage pipe will direct run-off into the desired area. Trevera construction cloth, which allows unhindered water flow but no transference of soil, lines the trench with enough excess at the top to overlap the trench. A rigid, perforated, plastic drain line is laid in the trench bottom and covered with clean, crushed stone or pea gravel. Folding the excess Trevera cloth over the top prevents soil from entering the trench. Hide the trench with mulch, stepping stones, or grass sod.

Natural run-off channels can be converted into a stream that redirects water from the pond. The channel should be deepened enough to accommodate construction as well as the progressive one inch per ten feet required for drainage. Concrete construction or pond liner material is camouflaged with various sizes of rocks and plants. Lining the channel with pea gravel should be avoided to prevent sediment accumulation. If the run-off occurs from a specific site, a debris-collecting screen can be located at the water entry point.

As a precaution against the toxic effects of chemical run-offs entering the pool, do not use insecticides, herbicides, and pesticides in the lawn areas around the pond or in the higher elevations from the pool. Even small doses of such chemicals can be harmful to both fish and plants.

RAINFALL FLOODING

The most common way to handle rainfall flooding is to have one section of the pool edging slightly lower.

*P*roviding a retaining wall up-slope from the pond redirects surface run-off away from the pond.

Plantings in this area should not object to occasional flooding. The overflow area may be designed as an actual bog garden, but it will require additional water during dry periods. Installing a bog garden within the confines of the pool liner, with stone separating the earth area from the pool area, will absorb most pond overflows. However, heavy rainfall areas may still require redirection of excess water away from the pond area.

A section of the edging may be dismantled to accommodate flexible black tubing installed at the desired maximum water level. The tubing is buried at a deepening depth of one inch per ten feet away from the pool to the selected drainage location. A screen should be placed across the tubing to prevent loss of fish. Daylilies (*Hemerocallis* sp.) planted at the site will enjoy the occasionally damp conditions as well as help hide the construction.

An adaptation of the standpipe, or vertically set pipe, may be used by connecting a non-toxic, silicone-sealed elbow joint to a drain line extending through the side wall of the pool. Since most liner adhesives require a professional-grade heat application for maximum strength, single-component silicone is an appropriate alternative. (See Chapter 5, "Adhesives and Sealants," pages 36–37.) Plants can be placed near the standpipe for camouflage.

See also Chapter 2, "Deteriorating Edges," pages 19–20, and Chapter 12, "Canadian Tips," pages 145–146.

UNDERGROUND WATER PRESSURE

If the pool is installed in an area with a high water table, underground water pressure may stress and crack concrete. Liners set in the ground will "bubble" or be lifted. Weighting the liner down with pea gravel or other stone is not likely to hold the liner in place since the water pressure is quite strong. It may be necessary to install a drainage trench all the way around the pool. (See "Run-Off Contamination," pages 8–9.)

Concrete pools may be drained and a pressure relief valve installed in the pool bottom. Because anaerobic activity can produce the toxic gases of methane and hydrogen sulfide beneath the liner, a standpipe can be installed around the valve to prevent these gases from entering the pond water. At this time, there is no such solution for lined pools. However, Dave Smith, of Serenity Ponds and Streams, suggests a lawn irrigation pressure valve may be installed in the pool bottom in the area where the liner is lifted. (See Chapter 5, "Adhesives and Sealants," pages 36–37.)

The most drastic situation will require a complete reconstruction in order to create a drainage system beneath the pool. This system should involve both drainage pipes and an appropriately deep layer of smooth drainage rock. Generous padding should protect the liner from the rocks below.

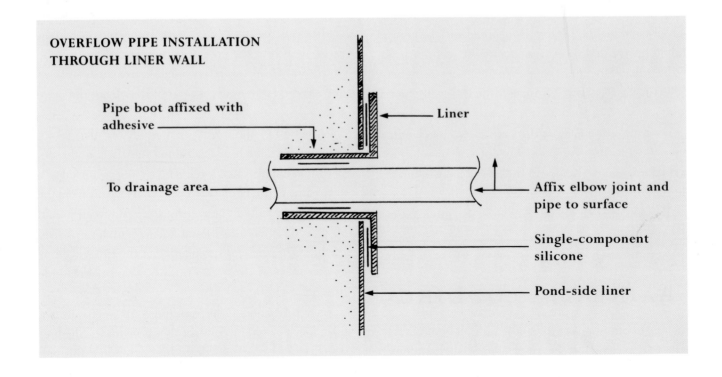

OVERFLOW PIPE INSTALLATION THROUGH LINER WALL

Pipe boot affixed with adhesive

Liner

To drainage area

Affix elbow joint and pipe to surface

Single-component silicone

Pond-side liner

*The overflow drainage pictured in the foreground is
well screened to prevent the loss of fish.*

*In a bubble effect, underground water pressure can
push up a liner.*

*Constructing a pond in a sloping area is accom-
plished with landscaped terracing.*

Mature trees growing askew to prevailing winds protect calm-loving water lilies.

Planting taller plants such as Iris pseudacorus on the windward pond edge will help protect water lilies.

STRONG WINDS

Strong winds create havoc with aquatic plants. A windbreak of shrubs or trees should be planted up-wind from the pond at a distance that will not allow shade or fallen debris to affect the pond. Because windbreaks create negative air pressure on the down-wind side that results in debris settling into the pond, they should be planted askew to the prevailing winds. Avoid deciduous trees, especially those with toxic leaves such as laburnum, holly, mountain laurel, rhododendron, yew, and horse chestnut. Likewise, pine needles and maple foliage will produce tannic acid, which not only discolors the water but may also stress or poison fish.

Taller ornamental grasses, such as miscanthus, can be planted at the pond's edge on the upwind side. Likewise, taller marginal plants, such as yellow flag water iris or reeds and rushes, placed on the upwind side of the pool will help protect the calm-loving water lilies.

The evergreen mountain laurel (Kalmia sp.), a striking shrub in bloom, has fish-toxic leaves and should not be planted poolside.

c h a p t e r   t w o

CONSTRUCTION

*The most carefully planned construction of a pond
can still present problems later on.*

Fibreglass, known for creating strong preformed ponds, can be designed to unique specifications and expressions.

PREFORMED POND CRACKS

Preformed ponds, especially plastics, can crack and split when exposed to winter freezes. A three-inch cushion of sand placed in the bottom of the excavation, as well as backfilled around the edges, will absorb the expansion created by ice. If minor cracking has occurred, the pool should be removed and appropriate sand cushioning provided. Several thin coats of neoprene rubber paint, allowed to dry fully between coats, will usually provide a proper repair.

PREFORMED POND NOT LEVEL

A preformed pool that is not set into its proper level of excavation will look unsightly and out of kilter, besides exposing the pool shell to degrading UV sunlight. Remove fish and plants to appropriate holding facilities, empty the pool, and remove it from the excavation. Be certain the soil base beneath the cushioning

sand is well tamped and level. Likewise, be certain the sand is level. Replace the pool and check that the upper edges are level. Fill the pond half full and check the level of the upper edges again. If the pool is level, tamp the backfill soil firmly around the sides, adding a generous layer of sand immediately next to the pool wall. Continue filling, tamping, and adding layers of sand. Replace the top edging, plants, and fish.

With the pond set slightly below ground level and bricks mortared around the edge, the underwater liner is protected from direct sunlight.

PREFORMED POND COLLAPSES

The use of heavy stone around a preformed pond can collapse the walls if much of the stones' weight rests on the edge of the pool. If the pool is repairable, remove it from the excavation and repair it. While the pool is removed, either construct a concrete collar around the pool (see "Deteriorating Edges," pages 19–20) or fill a one-foot-deep trench around the pool with first a generous layer of gravel and the remainder with concrete-stiffened soil.

LINED POND NOT LEVEL

For aesthetic reasons as well as for the prevention of UV damage to exposed liner material, it is important that the top edges of the pond be equally level. A carpenter's level used with solid boards that reach across the pool or a water line leveller from a building supply outlet can determine if the edges are properly levelled. It is always better to correct levelling by shaving off the soil at the higher points to avoid soft

*R*ainwater and surface drainage are prevented from entering the pond by setting the coping at an angle away from the pond.

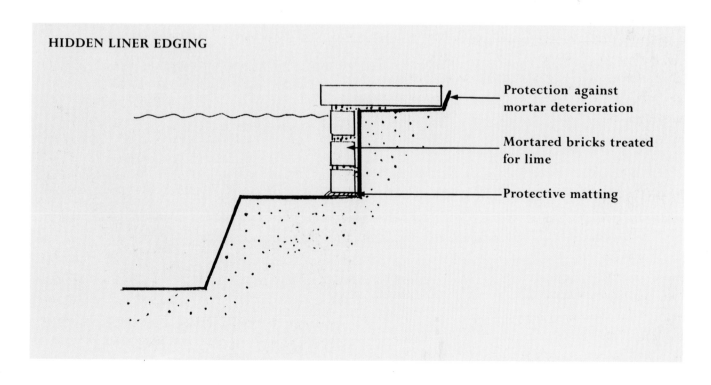

HIDDEN LINER EDGING

Protection against mortar deterioration

Mortared bricks treated for lime

Protective matting

areas that will settle in time. If an area must be built up, stiff concrete should be mixed in with the soil and the filling tamped firmly. If the soil lacks sufficient clay for a firm edge, a concrete collar (see "Deteriorating Edges," pages 19–20) or concrete-reinforced soil may need to be supplied completely around the pool.

Pond edges that extend into surrounding walkways provide the viewing area with stability.

TOXIC LINERS

Swimming pool liners and children's play pools are often treated with herbicides, biocides, and hydrocarbons to combat algae. All such chemicals will leech into the pond and eventually kill both fish and plants. Likewise, many roofing materials also contain toxic chemicals. Such liners should be replaced with a nontoxic material or the pond converted to a fountain-only display.

LEAKS IN LINED PONDS

Most manufacturers of pool liners provide patch kits or adhesive-backed tape that can repair small leaks. These repairs should be performed on warm, sunny days when the materials are more pliable. Some tapes require a heat application. Especially in the case of larger repairs, the heat provided by a hair dryer is insufficient. A professional heat blower may be re-

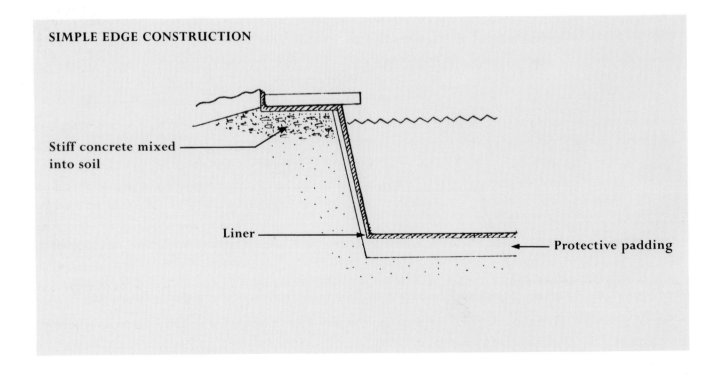

SIMPLE EDGE CONSTRUCTION

Stiff concrete mixed into soil

Liner

Protective padding

*P*ebbled concrete walkways firmly anchor the pond
edging and prevent deterioration.

quired for lasting repairs. Be very careful not to
stretch the liner or patch during the repair to avoid
weakening the area and making it vulnerable to a
recurring leak. For pin- or slash-type holes, a neoprene paint can be used.

Often, the greatest problem with leaks is simply
locating them. First, disconnect the waterfall to be
sure the leak is not occurring in that area. If the pool
water continues to lower, check that water is not
siphoning back out through the outlet tubing. Check
the corner folds of the liner for inner edges that may
have slipped down to allow leakage. Check the pool's

perimeter for edging that may have settled to create a
lower point. If none of these prove to be the source of
the leakage, it must be within the pool.

Joe B. Dekker, of the Waterscaping Company, reports an ingenious method of locating a leak within the
pool. Once it has been ascertained that the leak is
occurring within the pond, allow the water to leak to
its level. (Should the level be so low as to jeopardize
fish and plants, remove both to holding areas.) Once
the water has stabilized at a level, place two large
plastic containers in the pool and fill them with water.
This will slightly raise the water above the leak. Fill a

squirt-type bottle with milk and squirt a small bit at intervals around the pool perimeter a small way out from the edge. The milk will cloud into the water where there is no hole. Near the hole, the milk will move directly into the leak. The pool can then be drained below the leak and the hole repaired.

Another method of locating a leak is to slowly drain the pool so that the liner dries as the water level lowers. A hole in the side may darken with moisture as the leaked water returns through the hole. Since fabric underlay acts as a siphon, this method is not likely to be effective under such conditions.

If the hole is in the bottom of the pool, remove all fish and plants to safe quarters. Towels can be used to sop up the last water in the pool bottom. If the hole has been caused by something from within the pool, normal repairs can be executed. However, if the hole has been caused by a rock from beneath the liner, it will be necessary to remove the liner, properly clear the excavation, and supply a sufficient padding of sand, news-papers, or matting material.

If the underlay must be replaced, Joe Dekker suggests a good half inch of newspaper. As the newspaper decomposes in time, it becomes powdery, much like flour. And like flour, the gley repels water rather than siphoning it through a small hole. When laying newspaper in an excavation, a light hose-spraying prevents the paper from blowing about.

LEAKS IN CONCRETE PONDS

Repairs to concrete should not be performed in very cold or in very hot weather. Frost can damage the finish, and hot weather may cause the concrete to dry too quickly and lose strength. The area around the patching should be roughened to allow better adhesion. For maximum hardness, concrete should be allowed to cure slowly over a period of a week's time.

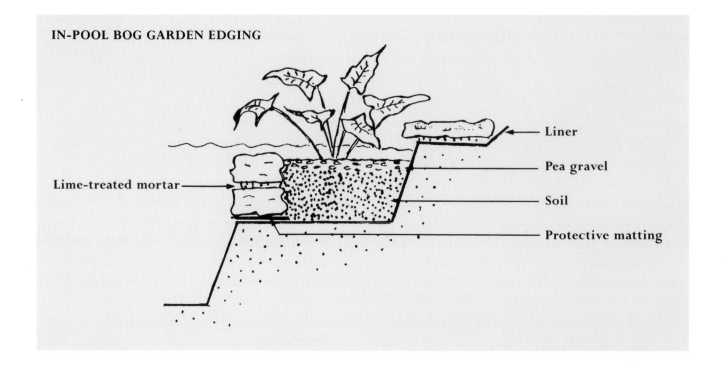

IN-POOL BOG GARDEN EDGING

Lime-treated mortar

Liner

Pea gravel

Soil

Protective matting

The reinforced substrata of flagstone paving prevents the pond edging from settling into the ground.

Spraying lightly with a hose will prevent too quick a drying as will a covering of several layers of well-soaked burlap. A stiff concrete mix will begin to harden fairly quickly and can actually complete the process under water. Concrete repairs should be treated with sealants or leeching procedures.

Always check the water's pH after concrete repairs. A reading over 8.5 indicates a toxic lime situation. Tetra-acetic acid or vinegar may be used in filling and refilling to clear the concrete lime from the water. Do not replace fish and plants until the water has been rendered safe. Several commercial lime-cure treatments are available, among them waterproofing sealants that penetrate masonry, caulking crack fillers, and neoprene rubber paint.

DETERIORATING EDGES

Deterioration of the pool edging may occur from moisture in the surrounding soil that allows the edge

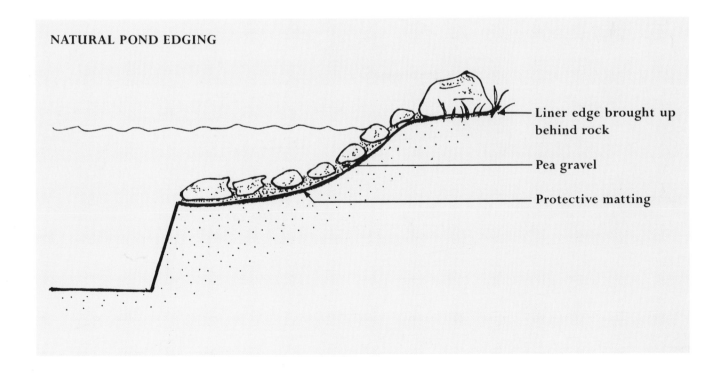

NATURAL POND EDGING

Liner edge brought up behind rock

Pea gravel

Protective matting

to settle, from porous soil composition that cannot support heavy rocks, or from heavy stone that is used with a deep or straight-sided pond. The edging should be carefully removed to prevent bits of mortar or concrete from falling into the pool. A concrete collar, concrete-reinforced soil, or hidden liner construction will effect repairs.

To construct a concrete collar, drain the pool and place fish and plants in appropriate temporary quarters. Carefully fold the liner to the inside of the pool. Make a wooden form for the collar to accommodate 6 to 12 inches of concrete at a width of 18 to 36 inches. Excavate the pool edges to these dimensions, taking care to keep the excavation base perfectly level. Flex-ible plastic can be used for curves in the pool's edge. If the collar is poured in sections, be sure to roughen the edges to allow strong adhesion. Keep the collar moist and allow it to cure properly. If the pool edging is wider than one or two stones, installing a concrete collar at the pool edge and then laying a generous hard core of stone in the adjacent area will prevent the stonework from shifting downwards.

Unstable capstones and the liner edge can be embedded in a trench of concrete installed a few inches from the pool edge. The concrete can be reinforced with steel mesh or Rebar®. If the edging stone is not too heavy, a 2- to 4-inch layer of stiff cement may be worked into the soil for increased stability.

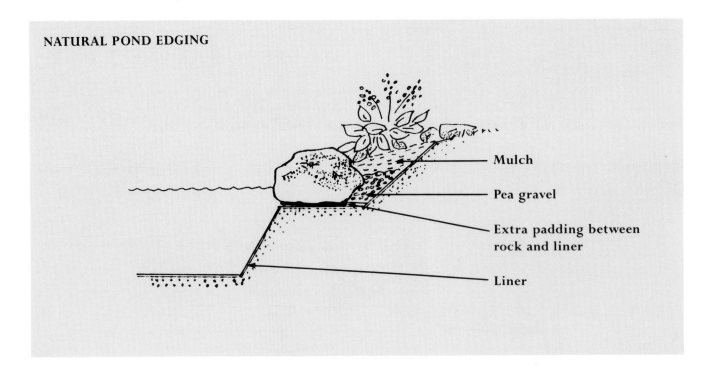

NATURAL POND EDGING

Mulch

Pea gravel

Extra padding between rock and liner

Liner

chapter three

WATERFALLS

*To prevent leaking, the entire waterfall is lined
with the liner edges extending above the flowing
water level.*

WATER LOSSES

Obviously, waterfalls constructed by simply stacking stones will leak water unless the entire feature is lined with a piece of pool liner. Likewise, waterfalls that are constructed of cemented stonework must also be lined as the cement may crack in cold climates. The liner should extend a bit above the highest water level as well as generously overlap the pool liner. This will accommodate the natural settling of the excavation spoil that is often used for waterfall features.

Any rocks placed on the liner material should have a second piece of liner provided to prevent punctures. It is also wise to provide an underlay of newspaper, sand, or matting beneath the entire liner. Should the waterfall be losing water from such punctures, it should be reconstructed to prevent future damage once the hole has been repaired.

Be certain water loss is not occurring due to faulty connections in the hosing from the pump. A non-toxic silicone sealant may be required. Another cause of water loss is fabric matting beneath the waterfall liner that overlaps the pond liner, touching and siphoning the pool water. Occasionally, tubing may also be sited so that it siphons water when the pump is not running.

Plants within the waterfall basin may divert water out the sides. Either the basin must be deepened or the sides restructured, including protective lining, to retain the water within the desired channel.

DISAPPEARING WATER

Spaces among the stones of the waterfall can provide secret places of water escape. While cement or mortar can be used to fill in these gaps, the remedy may be temporary since cement will crack in freezing weather.

Spray foam, available from hardware or building supply stores, can be forced into crevices to seal them for a much longer period of time. As the spaces are filled, the foam should be quickly pushed back into the crack since the product hardens in seconds. Joe Dekker recommends tossing a handful of sand onto the foam before it hardens to camouflage the white foam. The product can then be painted a neutral color with a non-toxic latex paint. The product can also be used to totally fill in behind rocks in the structure. Larger quantities are available for professional application.

WET WALLS

Since water forms a progressively narrower stream the farther it falls and is also drawn back towards its source, waterfall plateaus that are spaced too far apart will produce a trickling wet wall. To leave the waterfall structure as it is, it will be necessary to increase the pumping capacity. A larger-size hose may accomplish this, or it may be necessary also to upgrade the pump. Use a one-gallon bucket to pour water over the structure. Determine how many seconds it takes to empty the bucket to obtain the desired effect. Figure the gallons per hour needed and compare this with the pump and hose charts to determine the proper pump and tubing size needed for the desired effect.

Another solution is to reconstruct the waterfall. As it is rebuilt, allow the water being recycled through the hose to flow over the structure. Check the flow with each additional layer added to the structure.

EXCESSIVE FLOW

Clamps can be placed on the tubing to diminish the flow. These clamps should be placed on the outlet side of the pump and not tightened more than halfway to prevent stressing the pump. Likewise, the water force may be stemmed by attaching a tee connection to the

Allowing the water to flow directly out the hose over the falls can produce too strong a flow.

large basin at the ground level of the falls will spread the entry force of the water, especially if the lip is widened. This basin can be several inches deep. Pea gravel can be used to fill the basin to aid in adjusting water flow. Plants that enjoy moving water, such as watercress (*Nasturtium officinale* and *Cardamine cordifolia*), can be planted in the pea gravel basin. Such a planting absorbs some of the water flow and makes it appear the water is emerging from a hidden source, besides providing natural bio-filtration and salad greens. This remedy has the added benefit of the

pump, diverting some of the flow to a spouting ornament at the pool's edge or to a small fountain tucked in a corner where it will not disturb the water lilies.

Often the pump outlet provides for a size of tubing that is a narrow diameter. This can produce too strong a pressure. Installing a bushing increase adapter to allow the use of a larger diameter hose will reduce the force of the water flow. This is frequently advised, if only to produce a softer flow from the waterfall outlet.

If the opposite pool side is at least ten feet from the waterfall and the pump has been sited at the base of the waterfall, the water force may be stemmed by attaching a long enough hose to move the pump to that farther point. Ten feet of hose will add one foot to the lift load of the pump and decrease the pumping capacity accordingly.

If the face of the waterfall is too steep, the water may crash into the pond, creating cloudy water and unhappy lilies. The structure may need to be rebuilt to allow a more gradual entry into the pool. Likewise, a

A top basin at the water entry point ensures a gentle flow over the falls.

harder water flow above the basin being audible while the flow into the pool itself is lessened to a minimum more agreeable to water lilies.

INADEQUATE FLOW

The most obvious solution is to implement a larger capacity pump. Before replacing the pump, follow the procedure described in the Appendix and consult the pump chart to determine the size pump required at the waterfall's lift to achieve the desired effect.

If the pump is connected to a long hose run, the pump's efficiency may be hampered by friction within the hose. The pump may need to be relocated closer to the waterfall to decrease this friction. The hosing may be too narrow, especially if it has been fitted to the pump's existing outlet. A bushing adapter will allow a larger diameter of hose to be used.

Other water features, such as spouting ornaments that have been attached to the waterfall pump with a tee connection, can be disconnected and provided with a separate pump. A separate pump may also be required to accommodate the specific flow required of a bio-filter if the waterfall effect is inadequate.

WATERFALL EFFECTS

See the Appendix for a procedure to estimate the desired GPH and the corresponding pump capacity chart. Generally, 100 GPH of pump capacity will be needed per inch of spillway width at the discharge point. Physical adjustments can be made to the waterfall to gain the desired effect:

• The rocks the water flows over should be slanted downwards slightly to discourage diversion and backflow.

A wide lip to the waterfall spreads the force of the water flow.

• Sound and movement are increased by extending the lip or pond entry beyond the face of the structure.
• A wider sheet of water can be achieved by building a basin behind the spillway stone.
• Water can be made to appear to originate from several sources by attaching a manifold of PVC piping with branch lines adjusted by ball valves.
• Create a smooth edge to spillway rocks by adhering strips of plastic or fiberglass to the rock.
• A smooth edge may also be created by sculpting cement onto the rock. This method can be used when joining two or more rocks to create a single wide lip. Appropriate drying time must be allowed or the cement will quickly crumble away. Likewise, the cement should be sealed or treated to prevent lime from entering the pool. Non-toxic latex paint can be daubed onto the cement to give it the appearance of natural stone.
• A more natural and gentle flow from the top of the falls is achieved by constructing a leakproof wall or

barrier behind the hose's outflow. Direct the water back towards the wall rather than having it gush forward.

• Another method of achieving a gentle flow is to attach a perforated section of tubing to the outlet at the top of the waterfall. The perforations may be made on only one side of the tubing and that side stabilized away from the pool.

A tee attachment to the pump allows both a waterfall and a fountain to operate from the same pump and reduces the water flow to each.

Water is naturally drawn back to the waterfall face the longer it must drop to the next level.

Whiskey barrel tub gardens can be equipped with a small pump that recycles water through a spouting ornament or over a lava rock waterfall. These gardens should be fitted with a liner to prevent residual toxins from leeching into the water.

chapter four

SAFETY

The use of extension cords to operate the pump should never be more than a temporary measure.

ELECTRICITY

Electrical circuitry must be protected by a ground fault circuit interrupter or a suitable residual current circuit breaker with a 30 mA, 30 millisecond rating. Electrical outlets should be over 4 feet from the pool and equipped with weatherproof covers. Provisions are available to lock the cord in the outlet to prevent accidental disconnection.

Do not use indoor extension cords. Outdoor extension cords should be used only as emergency or short-term measures. Electrical cords should be protected by armor or protective conduit. Never handle any electrical apparatus without first disconnecting it.

If the pond fish seem agitated or you feel a tingling sensation when touching the water, immediately shut off any electricity to the pool.

POND LIGHTING

Low-voltage lights are safer and less expensive to operate than high-voltage lights. Lights must be wa-terproof and designed for use in and around water. Always use properly rated fuses and transformers. Site any junctions, even though they may be waterproof, above water if possible. If more than one light is used, purchase lights apart from their transformers. A single transformer may be used to accommodate several lights. The total wattage should be between fifty and one hundred percent of the transformer's rating. Use the largest gauge cable possible to minimize potential power loss between the transformer and appliance.

When a light burns out, shut off the electricity. Check for corrosion where the lamp enters the socket. Return water seals to their proper position when replacing bulbs to keep internal connections dry. Clean lamps regularly to prevent algae growth.

CONSTRUCTION

Prevent possible slipping and falls around the pool by abrading any potentially slippery surfaces. Provide drainage around the pond to avoid puddles.

Any loose stones or slabs around the pool should be solidly fixed to support an adult's weight safely.

Provide handrails where bridges are narrow or high above the water, where people might stand to view the pool, or where the pool is sited immediately off a deck or patio. Handrails should be spaced closely enough to prevent small children from falling through and should also be strong enough to support an adult's weight.

If stepping stones go out into the pool, provide a firm base so the stones do not tip or rock. Avoid porous stone that might disintegrate easily or become slippery with moss or algae.

Areas of the pool that are visited by viewers should be kept shallow. Large stones or treated concrete blocks can enclose an area to be filled with pea gravel, in effect creating a sort of beach that may prove

Lighting units may be effectively and safely concealed around the pond.

Stepping stones across the pond should be firmly set and far enough above the water level to avoid their becoming wet and slippery.

attractive to the area's birds. Low-growing aquatics can be grouped in such an area to act as a physical barrier while not obstructing the view of the pool.

GENERAL SAFETY

Post a warning of the pond's presence on the property where visitors can read it.

Water-soaked potted plants or stonework can be quite heavy. Lift them properly to avoid debilitating back strain.

Before using any chemical or medication, be aware of any safety hazards or toxicity. Even the most commonly available treatments may have critical precautions. There are many listings of precautions for medications and chemicals that the pool-owner might consider using. The local public library can often supply such information.

Although bacteria and pond parasites are not, as yet, known to trouble humans, it is still wise to bathe and scrub one's fingernails after working in the pond.

CHILDREN

An unsupervised child around a pond is not a safe situation. If the child falls into the pool, the owner is usually legally responsible. Keep life preservers on hand for young children's protection. Advise any visitors with small children of the pond's presence so they may exercise extra care in watching their children.

Since children seem to have an instinct for throwing objects into water, plants and fish may be harmed or destroyed. For the sake of both the children and the pool, the pond should be securely fenced or covered with strong steel mesh. Floating alarms are available that signal the water's disturbance; however, frogs and toads may keep it sounding constantly.

If shallow plant shelves that can function as an escape route from the pond are not present, sturdy pedestals should be set strategically around the pond. The plants set upon these pedestals may also discourage access by children.

All drugs and chemicals used to treat water or fish can be dangerous; keep them away from children.

A pond set adjacent to a patio or a deck will require special attention when children are present.

chapter five

PUMPS AND FILTRATION

*Employing even three pumps, the extended system
of outlets in this construction keeps the water flow
gentle enough for a water lily collection.*

DECREASED FLOW

Most submerged pumps are equipped with a small screen or mechanical filter to protect the pump's interior from debris. While a good hygiene program will keep such debris to a minimum, the screen can still become clogged and require a good hosing. In the spring it may be necessary to clean the filter once a week, while in the summer cleaning may be required only once every two or three weeks. Provide a larger screening area for the pump. The pump can be wrapped in a large piece of fiberglass window screen and then placed inside a larger, well-perforated plastic container.

The pump will clog faster if it is set on the pool bottom, where debris settles. Elevate the pump so that it is not continually pulling such debris. This debris can be vacuumed when performing partial water changes.

Be certain the hose is not twisted or being crushed by a rock or pot. Spirally reinforced hosing will provide greater stability. Elbow bends in the plumbing decrease pump efficiency and can be replaced by flexible black tubing. Even so, the hosing may become clogged with algal growth. This can happen with clear vinyl tubing. Use black hose or PVC piping.

Water may be leaking from hose connections. Fit all connections with stainless steel or ring-shaped fittings. A single-component silicone sealant will prevent leaking. (See "Adhesives and Sealants," pages 36–37.)

EXCESSIVE FLOW

See Chapter Three, "Excessive Flow," pages 22–24.

CORROSION

Pump housings are sometimes made of aluminum that will corrode in pond water. Attach a sacrificial anode to the pump. The anode will oxidize first and can be replaced at less expense than replacing a corroded pump. Avoid placing two different metals close to one another in the pool water since the softer metal will corrode. For example, iron fittings should not be used with an aluminum pump housing. Corroding metals are also toxic to fish.

Copper, brass, and bronze are corroded by the acetic acid emitted by single-component silicone sealant/adhesives. If using such sealant/adhesives, select plastic or stainless steel fittings or use the more expensive, odorless, single-component silicone that does not contain acetic acid.

OVERHEATING

A clogged filter screen may reduce water flow to such an extent that the pump is denied the cooling effect of

*A**llowing a pump to become dirty may stress, overheat, and damage it.*

the water flow. An overheated pump may burn out or the bearings may be damaged. Monitor the filter screen and hose it clean as necessary.

The pump will overheat if it is allowed to run dry, for example, when the pool is drained or when the filter screen becomes totally clogged. Never leave the pump unattended when draining the pond. Once the water level is low enough that air is being pulled through the pump, shut off the pump and complete the drainage by sopping the final water with towels.

FILTER CLEANING

If the unit must be cleaned more than once a week, it is too small for the pool. Install a larger unit or set up additional units.

Filtration media may be too fine and clog quickly. If the unit is large enough, replace some of the finer media with larger, textured media, such as baffles, netting, or brushes. Install a large screen area around the filter to trap larger particles.

If a swimming pool filter is used, it should be backwashed once a week. The sand should be stirred by hand to loosen debris and to work it to the surface. Air blowers can be installed to aid this process. Media should be #12 silica sand or pea gravel. Channelling is a common problem with these filters.

Channelling occurs when the water flows around the sides of the media rather than across it. The filtration media may be too fine or the water may be entering the filter at too great a pressure. In the latter case, a larger-diameter hose may be required.

Upflow filter units should have a bottom drain apart from the valve, recycling connections to the pump and water feature. To clean the filter unit, shut off the pump and close the valves to prevent dirty water from re-entering the pool. Use a garden hose to force water down through the media, where it will exit out the bottom drain. Hose grates thoroughly to clean off algae. If such cleaning is performed regularly, it will not be necessary to dismantle the unit for cleaning during the season. This cleaning method is not effective if the filter contains various sizes of gravel as they will mix together and diminish the filter's capacity.

Downflow filters will have most of the debris in the top layer of media. A drain should be provided above the media level in the top of such filters. Shut off the pump and close the pool-return valves before using a hose to add water to the filter unit. Stir up the top layer of media to loosen any trapped sediment and allow it to flow out the drain.

Air blower systems are useful for cleaning gravel-type filtration units. PVC piping is drilled with small holes and faced downwards into the media. The piping is connected to an air blower that causes the dirt to be backwashed up and out a top drain in the filter unit.

INADEQUATE BIO-FILTRATION

Bio-filters remove dissolved organic wastes from pool water. They use nitrosonomas and nitrobacter bacteria to convert ammonia into nitrite and then into nitrate. Bio-filters are not used to remove algae from the water, nor do they function as mechanical filters for the removal of particulate debris. If water testing confirms the presence of ammonia in the pool, the bio-filter may not be performing adequately. Frequently, this is caused by an overstocking of fish. Before treating the problem, action should be taken to protect the fish, if necessary.

A bio-filter should be in operation twenty-four hours a day. A shutdown of only a few hours can result in the death of much of the bacteria. Aerobic bacteria must have a constant source of oxygen to survive. An

*B*lack submersible pumps (above) are less visible in
the pond.

A box-style filter (right) attaches to a submerged
pump to provide mechanical filtration of particulate
matter. In this assembly, the cleaned water returns
to the pond via a fountain head.

air-blower can provide oxygen during periods of shut-down or a large container of clean water can recycle through the filter. During normal operation, the oxygen supply within the filter may be enhanced with an air-bar at the water's entry.

The rate of water flow through the filter may be inadequate. One to two gallons per minute per square foot of filter surface should be pumped through the filter. The square footage of filter media surface required is determined by dividing the pool volume gallons by 125. For example, an 8 × 10 × 2 foot pool has a volume of approximately 1,200 gallons. Dividing this volume by 125 determines that approximately 10

square feet of filter media surface is required to service the pool. To determine the necessary pumping capacity, multiply the square footage of media surface by one and two and then each by 60 minutes. In this case, the required pumping capacity would be between 600 GPH and 1,200 GPH.

In conjunction with the flow rate, the pool volume should be turned over once every one to two hours for maximum effectiveness. If a pool has over 2,500 gallons, the turnover rate may be adjusted to once every 3 or 4 hours. This approximates half the pump capacity determined by the above process.

Using a hose of less than ¾ inch in diameter will

*W*atercress **(Nasturtium officinale),** *a lover of moving water, aids in bio-filtration when grown in the path of the water's entry.*

lessen the bio-filter's effectiveness as it restricts the water flow to the filter. A large pool may require an even larger-size hose.

A bio-filter will not function in temperatures below 55°F. If the pool is not overstocked, ammonia production is not likely to present a problem at lower temperatures when the fish's metabolism is slowed. In the early spring, however, before the water has stabilized above 55°F and the fish are resuming activity, the ammonia level should be monitored closely until the bacteria have been able to resume working.

A new or restarted bio-filter may require as much as three or four months to become established naturally. Seeding the bio-filter with bacteria may alter the time frame to one or two weeks. While some people consider present research on such effectiveness to be inconclusive, there is evidence that seeding the filter will have some degree of impact, depending upon which commercial brand is used. Nevertheless, monitor the ammonia and nitrite levels of the pond water to determine the filter's effectiveness. During the initial phase, nitrite levels may rise until the nitrobacter

bacteria bring the conversion of nitrite to nitrate under control. Since nitrite is toxic to fish and even small amounts will stress them, it is important to take measures of protection. (See Chapter 6, "Nitrite," pages 45–46.)

Commercial bacteria products are available in both air-dried and liquid form. The air-dried form is preserved in a dormant state and becomes active when added to warm, dechlorinated water that is supplied with aeration. Under proper storage conditions, it may have a shelf life of two years.

Because the bacteria need nutrients and oxygen to survive, liquid forms may have a shelf life of only two months. If seeding with such products does not appear to have an impact when all other conditions are met, it may be because the product has exceeded its shelf life. Seeding a bio-filter with bacteria should be done in the late afternoon when the pool's oxygen content is highest. It is still helpful to provide additional aeration.

Pond medications and chlorinated water will kill the bacteria and require a new start-up. Do not clean the filter with a strong force of water or with chlorinated tap water. Monitor the ammonia content of the water following even 5 to 10 percent water changes. Because municipal suppliers may vary the amounts of chlorine and ammonia added to the water according to their perceived need, there may be fluctuations in the pool water. While small percentage water changes are unlikely to destroy all of the bacteria, a reduced efficiency may require appropriate steps to protect the fish.

Many municipal suppliers also add copper sulfate once or twice a year. Usually such additions are publicized in the local papers and frequently posted in pet stores. Since copper sulfate will destroy the bacteria, water changes of any dimension should not be effected during this period. It may be wise to have one or two large, plastic trash containers filled with good water as protection for emergencies.

Water entering the bio-filter should be adequately filtered of particulate debris to prevent such sediment from collecting on the media surface where it will suffocate the bacteria. Healthy bio-film layers are reddish to orange-brown in color and will smell earthy. Foul-smelling blackish color indicates a lack of oxygen and dying bacteria.

Since water must flow slowly through the media to accommodate the bacteria's activity, water returning to the pond may be seriously deprived of oxygen. Observe fish for signs of oxygen depletion and provide more if necessary. A simple aquarium air pump fitted with a diffuser bar may be sufficient.

Water pH should be between 6.5 and 7.8 for maximum efficiency of bacteria. Nitrification will not occur below 5.0 or above 9.0. Baking soda (sodium bicarbonate) or ground limestone (calcium carbonate) can be used to raise water pH. Mixing 2 teaspoons of vinegar with a bottle of water and dispersing it about the pond once a day will lower the pH. Changing the water pH by more than 0.2 during a 24-hour period is harmful to fish.

Different filter media appear in the marketplace each year. Review current retail catalogs, if only for ideas. At the time of this writing, the following media were being used:
- Pea gravel—Effective as a coarse filter medium, this can be heavy in any quantity.
- Angular gravel—Also heavy in quantity, the variation in shape lends to clogging.
- Volcanic or baked clay balls—While lightweight, these tend to float unless restrained.
- Brushes—These are most useful for pre-filtering.
- Plastic rings or hair-rollers—Relatively efficient for supplying adequate surface area, large quantities are required.
- Filter foam—Used most frequently as a pre-filter for granular media, it does require frequent cleaning and has a short life.
- Filter matting—Usually made of plastic or nylon fibres of a coarser nature and longer life than the foam, they still require frequent cleaning.
- Zeolite—Alumina-silicate rocks that absorb ammonia and normally require recharging every five to six weeks in salt baths. They may be placed in nylon stockings to facilitate removal and recharging. (See Chapter 6, "Ammonia," pages 44–45.)
- Activated carbon—Placed in nylon stockings for ease of cleaning and recharging, this medium is effective for the removal of medications and organic pollutants. (See Chapter 6, "Activated Carbon Adsorption," page 47.)

SUSPENDED SOLIDS

Aluminum sulfate or common alum, available at most pharmacies, will precipitate suspended clay particles from the water to the pond's bottom where they may be vacuumed. Mix a stock solution of one teaspoonful in a bucket of water and distribute about the pond. Repeat if necessary. Once the clay has settled to the pool bottom, it may be vacuumed out.

Well water especially may be plagued with high mineral contents, particularly iron. This will cause the water to appear cloudy immediately upon filling the pool. Commercial products or EDTA may be used to chelate out the minerals. (See Chapter 6, "Heavy Metals," page 41.) Providing good aeration will precipitate out the minerals, but will take longer. (See also "Filtration Alternatives," pages 37–38.)

Tannin flocculants cause suspended particles to coagulate so that they may be netted out with a fine mesh net or vacuumed after they have settled to the pool bottom. These products are especially useful for removing dying algae from the pool.

Up to twenty percent of non-chlorinated pool water may be vacuumed from the pond bottom where

*F*iltration media such as zeolite or activated carbon can be hidden inside this uniquely designed filtration/waterfall unit.

sediment has settled. If the water is chlorinated, replacing more than five to ten percent of the water mandates appropriate dechlorination. Pond vacuums are available or a large aquarium gravel vacuum will attach to a garden hose. These vacuums work on a siphoning principle and require the water at the tap to be running full force. By gently stirring bottom gravel, sediment is loosened for vacuuming or removal by the submerged pump. Aquarium vacuums should be pushed straight down into the gravel and gently lifted, the rock settling back down and the trapped sediment rising up into the tube for removal.

Settling chambers may be established outside the pool. The water velocity should be no more than one half foot per second to allow particles to settle to the bottom. Also, a surface area of one to two square feet per gallon per minute, or 120 square feet per gallon per hour, is recommended. Divide the 120 square feet per GPH into your pump's GPH capacity and double the answer to cut the velocity to one half. For a 600 GPH pump, 10 square feet of settling chamber would be required for the maximum efficient velocity. Settling chambers should be set up prior to a bio-filter or

suitably camouflaged at the back of a waterfall return or beneath decking.

FILTRATION OF GREEN WATER ALGAE

Very fine foam will remove suspended green water algae. However, frequent cleaning is required. It is important to implement other means of algae control as mechanical filtration control may be impractical for the season's duration.

A filter can be adapted to lessen green water algae effects by using a layer of wheat or barley straw. The straw should be confined in nylon bags since they will require changing every two to three weeks before they begin to rot and pollute the water. The use of straw during the winter is a recognized deterrent to spring algae blooms.

See "Filtration Alternatives," pages 37–38.

ADHESIVES AND SEALANTS

It may be necessary to use a sealant or adhesive with the fittings of submerged pumps and filters. Rubber-based sealants are effective in most cases, but do not afford good adhesive qualities. As has been mentioned previously, multiple-component silicones, epoxies, and superglues will attack and degrade plastics and liner materials.

Single-component silicone provides a durable, moisture-resistant sealant and adhesive for plastics. However, the acetic acid contained in most commonly available single-component silicones is corrosive to brass, copper, and bronze. Neutral cure silicones that do not emit the corrosive acid are available but are more expensive and need longer curing periods. As a sealant, a minimum of 24 hours' exposure to air and humidity is required. As an adhesive, the bonding cure may require a week's exposure to air and humidity. A ⅛- to ¼-inch-diameter bead of silicone achieves maximum strength. Thicker layers require more drying time and are weaker.

Silicone is not recommended for use on concrete or mortar or in the presence of saltwater.

FILTRATION ALTERNATIVES

Richard Schuck, of Maryland Aquatic Nurseries, offers what he calls the Ten Percent Solution, based on the natural concept of a pond-within-a-pond. Offering an area equal to ten percent of the total pool surface, the "inside" pool is either a preform pool or is constructed of pressure-treated lumber and a flexible liner at a depth of 12 to 18 inches. At the opposite side from the water entry point, an overflow provision allows particle settlement as the water passes over pots of marginal plants. Watercress (*Nasturtium officinale* and *Cardamine cordifolia*), a lover of moving water, may be placed at the water's entry. Floating plants such as water hyacinth (*Eichhornia* sp.) and water lettuce (*Pistia* sp.) help to remove wastes from the water. Plant roots and the gravel pot-topping serve as surface area for the colonization of nitrifying bacteria. Mr. Schuck recommends that a submerged foam filter also be used to maintain biological function during plant dormancy.

Joe B. Dekker's surface skimmer filtration system uses a large, heavy-duty, square plastic trash container. A 4″ × 9″ flap opening is cut near the top and reinforced with pop-riveted 1 × 2 wood strips. An extension of the pool liner is also riveted to the folded-in flap where hooks are mounted to hold a mesh

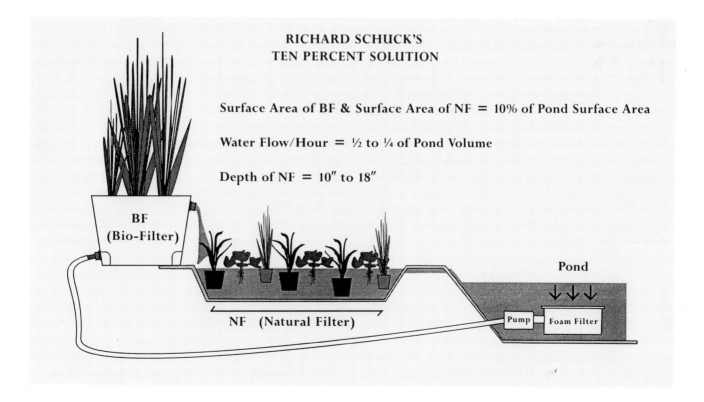

RICHARD SCHUCK'S TEN PERCENT SOLUTION

Surface Area of BF & Surface Area of NF = 10% of Pond Surface Area

Water Flow/Hour = ½ to ¼ of Pond Volume

Depth of NF = 10″ to 18″

BF (Bio-Filter)

NF (Natural Filter)

Pond

Pump   Foam Filter

laundry bag. A submersible pump on the container's bottom pumps the water through a 1¼″ plastic hose that is buried around the pond's perimeter to the waterfall on the opposite side. Canned foam, available from hardware stores, is sprayed on the container's lid and painted to look like stone. The inner mesh bag may be removed for dumping the debris that is pulled into the filter unit from the pool's surface.

Clair Henley, of Wychwood Carp Farm in England, shares an English method used to clear green water algae while the submerged plants are becoming established. One-inch-diameter holes are cut in one half the bottom of a large plastic trash container so that water may return to the pond when the container is set on the pond's edge. The container is filled halfway with old pantyhose or nylon stockings and a piece of foam fitted to the midway diameter of the container. A rock prevents the mechanical filter from tipping into the pool. A piece of cloth is draped over the top, while the hosing from the pump is rerouted to the container. The stockings and foam need to be hosed clean once or twice a day, but the method clears the water in a short time. By attaching a spray-bar to the hose, aeration is created that also removes heavy minerals from the water.

INEFFECTIVE UV STERILIZER

A UV sterilizer may seem to be ineffective if too much is expected of the unit. It may take a full week or two to clear the water of algae. The unit does not remove the algae from the water, it simply kills them. UV rays are relatively short and will penetrate but a few inches. If the water is especially green, the rays may not be able to penetrate deeply enough to effect a rapid clearing. Mechanical filtration or vacuuming the dead algae must be performed to prevent unsightly sediment buildup and a recurrence of the algae bloom from the added nutrients of decomposing dead algae.

Since the UV unit treats only what passes through it, it will not effect control of filamentous algae. Likewise, it will not remove suspended particles or ammonia and nitrite. Nor should it be expected to control the rapid propagation of disease-causing bacteria and parasites.

To maintain the specific temperature range that is required for optimum efficiency, a quartz sleeve must be installed between the bulb and the water. Maximum efficiency also requires a particular flow rate of water. A PVC tee with a ball valve will control the flow through the unit. Do not exceed the manufacturer's suggested flow rate as decreased efficiency will only result. Regular cleaning of the unit is necessary for maintaining efficiency. The bulb should be replaced each season.

chapter six

WATER QUALITY

*Beautiful water lilies, such as this "Attraction,"
require good water quality if they are to flourish
and remain healthy.*

CHLORINE AND CHLORAMINES

Chlorine and chloramines are harmful to fish and will kill the beneficial nitrifying bacteria in the pool. Likewise, they may burn or kill aquatic plants. Chlorine, a volatile gas, will dissipate with water circulation and exposure to the air within one or two days. Chloramines, however, take much longer to break down naturally. Municipal water suppliers are more frequently adding ammonia to combine with chlorine to produce the longer-lasting chloramines. It is not uncommon for municipal water to test positive for ammonia straight from the tap.

When adding chlorinated water to the pool, spray it in by hose to provide the necessary aeration for dissipation of the gas. Commercially prepared dechlor products are available from pet or pond supply stores. Some retail products claim also to break down chloramines. In the case of only five to ten percent water additions, it is unlikely the resulting ammonia from the treatment will affect fish. (In the case of new products that convert toxic ammonia to its non-toxic form, NH_3 to NH_4, testing will remain positive for ammonia.) However, greater water changes and possible varying concentrations added by the supplier merit testing of the water following dechlorination treatments.

Sodium thiosulfate will remove chlorine from water. A stock solution of four ounces of sodium thiosulfate crystals to one gallon of distilled water is prepared. One drop of stock solution per gallon of pool water is then used. Sodium thiosulfate will also pull the chlorine from the chloramine. Monitor ammonia levels. Label and safely store the solution.

As a precautionary measure, if the pool is regularly topped off or changed 5 to 10 percent weekly with chlorinated water, setting up filtration through one pound of zeolite per 100 gallons of pool water will help

Bubbles collecting on the water indicate the presence of organic decomposition.

to remove residual ammonia. Recharge the zeolite overnight every few weeks. A well-functioning biofilter will also remove such amounts of ammonia.

Up to five percent of the pool's water can be replaced with untreated chlorinated water no more than once or twice weekly without harming fish or plants. If nitrifying bacteria are being relied upon, such an addition may harm them. The water should be tested for ammonia and nitrite a couple of days after the water addition to determine their rising presence, which can occur if the bacteria have been destroyed. Reseeding the pool's bacteria should be performed only after the added chlorines and chloramines have been removed.

HEAVY METALS

Well water may contain ferrous bicarbonate, detected by a brown precipitate that forms when neutral or alkaline water is aerated. Besides being mildly irritating to fish, ferrous bicarbonate stains equipment and causes the water to appear cloudy. Manganese zeolite can be used to filter out the iron if the concentration is not high. Higher iron concentrations can be removed by aerating the water and passing it through a mechanical filter. Precipitation will occur faster in warmer water.

EDTA (Ethylene-diamine-tetra-acetic acid) may be used to chelate heavy minerals such as iron and copper from the water. Extreme caution should be used when using such chemicals as the chelation of minerals from the water often results in rapid drops in the water pH.

Chelating, or removing heavy minerals from the water, will leave an unsightly coating on the pond sides and bottom.

The safest way to use EDTA is to make up a stock solution of one teaspoon of EDTA to four ounces of water. Fill a two-gallon pail with pool water and add two drops of the stock solution. The minerals will precipitate in a brownish sedimentation in the pail. Check the water pH before and after to determine the pH change effected by the two-drop dosage. If the pH has not been altered by the maximum of 0.2, another two drops may be added and the results tested. Once

the proper safe dosage has been determined, divide the pool volume in gallons by two to determine the appropriate daily dosage.

Using chemicals to remove heavy minerals from the water will immediately cloud the water. As the cloudiness disappears, an unattractive sedimentation remains throughout the pool. A pool vacuum will remove much of it, but may involve a significant lowering of the pond's water. A complete water change and thorough cleaning of the pool may be required. If the water used to fill the pool is the source of the heavy minerals, the entire procedure may prove to be impractical.

SUSPENDED CLAY PARTICLES

See Chapter Five, "Suspended Solids," pages 35–36.

CONTAMINATED WATER

Run-off water, water from a nearby stream, or collected rainwater may contain toxic insecticides, herbicides, or fertilizers. Rainwater that has passed over metal roofs or asbestos shingles will contaminate the pool and may prove toxic to both fish and plants. If fish display signs of toxicity, execute a fifty-percent water change and/or move the fish to safe quarters until the water has been changed.

"Acid rain" may produce stress in water lilies. Immediately following a heavy rainfall, the lily leaves may show signs of burning at the edges or abrupt yellowing. A partial water change may be needed after such rainy periods if pH readings are lower than the neutral 7.

White foam at the waterfall entry of the pool is a sign of a high level of dissolved organic compounds.

Cloudy, brown water from suspended clay particles detracts from the beauty of this water lily.

Plants such as this parrot's feather (Myriophyllum) cannot survive heavy sediment accumulations in an ill-tended pond.

Conduct a partial water change to dilute the dissolved organic level. Take steps to correct the cause of the organic overload. The primary causes of high levels of dissolved organics are overstocking of fish, overfeeding of fish, or decomposing wastes in the pool bottom. Activated carbon filtration will adsorb dissolved organics.

WATER pH

Confusion exists concerning the use of the terms "water hardness" and "water pH." Water hardness generally refers to the degree of presence of calcium carbonate ($CaCO_3$) and magnesium compounds in the water. It will be expressed as "parts per million" or "degrees of hardness" with one degree of hardness equal to 17.1 parts per million. A hardness of between 50 and 200 parts per million is considered acceptable for goldfish. On the other hand, pH refers to the degree of presence of hydrogen ions, measured on a logarithmic scale of 0 to 14. A pH value of 7 is considered neutral with higher values being considered alkaline and lower values being considered acidic. The pH range of 6 to 8.5 is acceptable for most pond life. The primary concern with pH is its direct relationship to the toxicity of ammonia and nitrite. Each pH integer above the neutral 7 reflects a tenfold increase in such toxicities.

The pH values below neutral are acidic. Baking soda (sodium bicarbonate) and ground limestone (calcium carbonate) will raise the pH level.

Indications of high pH conditions are usually noticed in fish behavior and plant growth. Fish are stressed at pH readings consistently over 8.5 and by changes of more than 0.2. Such stress can promote infections and diseases. Plant growth may be inhibited, and submerged aquatics may accumulate a whitish coating from excess calcium salts.

If green water algae is present, the pH reading will be lower in the early morning. These pH swings are tolerated by the usual pond fish for short periods of time. Correcting the green water algae problem will alleviate the pH swings. Adding buffers such as sodium bicarbonate or calcium carbonate to the pool water may prevent significant pH swings, although only with pool water testing on the low side of neutral.

A pH reading over 9 may signal imminent disaster for fish, since a pH reading of 10 is directly toxic. At such high pH readings, the most minimal presence of ammonia and nitrite will be lethal. Remove the fish to safer quarters or effect an immediate fifty-percent water change to dilute the ammonia and nitrite. (See Chapter Nine, "Ammonia and Nitrite," pages 107–108.) Once the fish have been tended, the cause of the high pH should be determined and treated.

Getting pH readings of 9 and above is probably because cement or mortar is leeching toxic lime into the water. Thoroughly remove all bits of mortar that may be in the pool; small bits may be siphoned out with a pool vacuum. Untreated concrete blocks used as plant pedestals may be a source of lime. Some

*S*upplemental aeration can be provided by a spouting water feature.

reconstituted materials used in the pool may be leeching lime and growing to toxic levels over a period of time. Cement dust blowing into the pool, deteriorating pool edging, and rainwater washing in leeched lime from mortar used in the pool's edging are other sources of increased lime levels. Treat any concrete sources with a commercial lime neutralizer or a non-toxic pool sealant paint.

Green water algae may compound the problem. If the water is so green as to prevent necessary visibility for removal of cement and mortar, the pool may need to be partially or totally drained. Removal of lime sources should be the primary concern. Do not return fish to the pool until the pH is under 8. If chemicals are used to lower the pH, they are best used in the absence of fish along with the removal of lime sources.

It is unlikely that the use of hard limestone in the pool edging, waterfall, or bottom of the pool will cause pH readings over 8.5. In fact, the presence of some limestone in the pool may act as a buffer to pH fluctuations by supplementing calcium salts removed from the water by plants. This is especially true if the pond water tends to be on the low side of neutral. Soft, crumbly limestone used in and around the pool can present a problem, although it is unlikely the problem will extend beyond an 8.5 pH reading.

If the pool is supplied by well water with a normally high pH, it is wise to select fish that are better acclimated to such readings. The fancy breeds of goldfish and orfe will not remain happy in such water. Common goldfish, shubunkin, comet goldfish, or koi can better tolerate higher, non-toxic levels.

If a bio-filter is used, you may notice the pH readings are higher once nitrification has begun. This does not create a problem situation, nor is it likely to effect significant pH elevations.

***D**warf sagittaria planted in the pea gravel lining of this pond ensure year-round water clarity.*

AMMONIA

Any ammonia present in the water will be stressful and may be fatal to fish. Low levels of ammonia over a period of time will leave a fish susceptible to infection and disease. Pool water should be tested for ammonia every one to two weeks. Any indication of ammonia should be monitored on a daily basis. Particularly in the presence of elevating pH, ammonia can quickly attain toxic levels and should be treated as an emergency situation for fish.

Ammonia can be removed from the water in several ways:

- Execute a fifty percent water change. Avoid stressing fish and plants by drastic temperature changes of water and chlorinated water. If necessary, move fish and plants to temporary safe quarters.
- Ion-exchange resins such as zeolite will absorb ammonia from the water for up to two weeks. Eight ounces per 500 gallons of pool water may be confined in nylon or mesh bags and suspended in the water. To recharge, soak the zeolite overnight in a solution of

one pound of non-iodized salt dissolved in three gallons of water.

- Zeolite may also be used as a filtration media. Normally available in gravel form, zeolite is now available in a larger rock size that may be used directly on the pool bottom. As ammonia is absorbed by the zeolite, nitrifying bacteria colonize on the surface of the rocks and feed upon the absorbed ammonia. This feeding removes ammonia, thereby freeing space for more ammonia absorption.

- Bio-filtration, in which nitrosonomas and nitrobacter bacteria use oxygen to convert ammonia into nitrite and then into relatively harmless nitrate, may require as much as eight weeks to become established enough to impact ammonia concentrations. Preserved bacteria can be used to "seed" the filter or pool to shorten the impact period to a week or two. (See Chapter Five, "Inadequate Bio-Filtration," pages 32–35.)

Well water, often high in dissolved iron, can appear a cloudy brown and leave unsightly staining on the pond liner.

- Aquarium Pharmaceuticals has patented a new product, Ammo Lock-2, which converts toxic ammonia (NH_3) into its non-toxic form (NH_4). Since the water continues to test positive for ammonia, monitor fish behavior for evidence of toxicity.

Once the ammonia has been rendered safe, the cause of the rise should be determined and treated. The most common cause of ammonia concentrations is an excess of fish in the pond. Because fish do grow and spawn, the stocking level can grow to exceed the pool's capacity. Excess fish should be relocated. Decaying organic matter such as excess fish food and dying vegetation also produces ammonia. If this is a contributing factor, the pool bottom can be vacuumed during the emergency water change. If a rise in pH has contributed to the toxic level of ammonia, the pool should be checked and cleared of lime sources.

NITRITE

If ammonia is present in the water, it is likely that nitrite will also be present. Nitrite is highly toxic to fish as it interferes with the fish's blood hemoglobin and causes suffocation. Any presence of nitrite in the pool water should be treated. A toxic level should be immediately treated by a fifty percent water change followed by the salt treatment described below. If necessary, remove fish to safer quarters until the pool water has been treated.

Adding either calcium chloride or sodium chloride will help to control nitrite toxicity. The addition of salt also benefits stressed fish. Either chloride may be added at the rate of 20 mg/l for each mg/l or ppm of nitrite tested in the pool. Test kits that give results in terms of total nitrogen can be converted to nitrite readings by multiplying by 3.28. The nitrite reading of mg/l is multiplied by 20 mg and then by the number of liters in the pool to determine the needed amount of salt. Generally, 2.5 pounds of non-iodized salt per 100 gallons of water will detoxify nitrite.

Since both ammonia and nitrite are invisible, it is wise to test the water regularly for their presence.

HYDROGEN SULFIDE

Hydrogen sulfide is a product of anaerobic decomposition of organic matter. Having a characteristic rotten-egg odor, it is toxic to fish and increases in toxicity with higher temperatures. Commonly present in well water, it may be removed by vigorous aeration. A dosage of 2 to 6 mg/l of potassium permanganate will also remove it.

If the hydrogen sulfide is being produced in the pool bottom, the decaying matter should be vacuumed from the pool. Vigorous aeration of the pool water should also be provided.

EXCESS CARBON DIOXIDE

Carbon dioxide is produced by plants during the dark hours of night, when their cells switch to aerobic respiration by the process of photosynthesis. An excessive amount of carbon dioxide in the water will interfere with a fish's ability to access oxygen. Frequently, excessive amounts of carbon dioxide in the water are related to insufficient amounts of oxygen. Also, carbon dioxide acts as an acid in water, which effects a lowering of the water's pH.

Aeration will drive excess carbon dioxide from the water. If fish are gulping at the water's surface early in the morning, it will be necessary to provide aeration throughout the night to both dissipate excess carbon dioxide and increase available oxygen.

Water in the pH range of 6.0 to 7.0 will be more susceptible to pH fluctuations caused by carbon dioxide concentrations.

OXYGEN DEPLETION

Low oxygen levels can result in the sudden death of an entire fish population as well as seriously impair the effectiveness of bio-filters. Additional aeration of the water should be provided. In a very small pool, a simple aquarium air pump fitted with an air stone or diffuser bar will suffice. A larger pool may require an electric air compressor in an emergency. The recycling pump can be redirected to spray returning water onto the water surface for maximum aeration.

Intentionally or accidentally shutting off the pump can reduce the amount of oxygen in the water. Especially in hot weather when water is less able to hold oxygen, the pump should remain aerating the pool 24 hours a day.

If the pool has become overstocked with fish, relocate the excess population.

Provide emergency aeration by placing the pump just below the water's surface. Screen water intake and move any water lilies from the immediate area.

Additional oxygen is required by fish for the digestion of food. During hot weather, fish should be fed during the cool of the day in smaller quantities than usual. If the pool is stocked to its capacity, it may be advisable not to feed fish at all during hot weather when the pool's oxygen capacity is lower.

Heavy rains, strong winds, or a quick onset of autumn may result in the pool water "turning." The bottom layer of the pool is cooler and contains less oxygen than the top layer, which has access to warmth and gas exchanges at the surface. Strong weather may disrupt the upper water layer and cause it to mix with the lower layer. Rapidly cooling temperatures that cool the upper layer and equalize the pool's temperature will also effect a transference of water layers. Pools that have no recycling are especially subject to water turning. Additional aeration should be provided if fish gasp at the surface.

Successive cloudy days will disrupt plant photosynthesis, resulting in less oxygen being released into the water during the day. Since carbon dioxide is produced at night, its production is not affected. The presence of green water algae can make these conditions critical since algae are photosynthetic plants. Additional aeration should be provided around the clock and steps taken to reduce the amount of green water algae, if necessary.

Following chemical treatments for algae, decomposition of the dying algae can seriously deplete oxygen levels. Mechanically filter the dying algae from the pool or use a flocculant to sink them to the pool bottom for vacuuming. Replacement water should be sprayed onto the pool's surface. Added insurance is provided by supplemental or 24-hour aeration.

Since oxygen enters the water where the water comes into contact with the air, too many surface plants can seriously handicap the exchange. An excess of plants can also use more oxygen during the night hours than they can readily replace during the day.

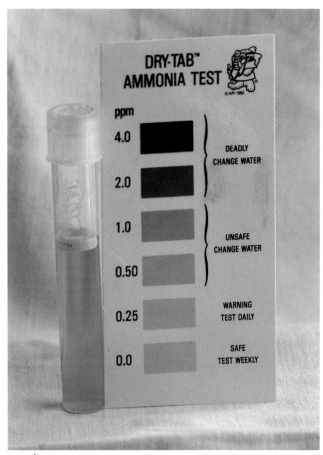

A municipally supplied water sample is tested directly from the tap to show an ammonia level dangerous to pond fish.

Excess surface plants should be removed and supplemental aeration provided as necessary.

ACTIVATED CARBON ADSORPTION

Activated carbon or charcoal may be used as a filter media to remove soluble organic matter, colloidal substances, some chemical treatments, and residual chlorine. This adsorption occurs more slowly in cold water. Its use will not change the water's pH. Use one pound per 100 gallons of pool volume. Rinse the carbon when it becomes coated with matter. The carbon may be rinsed four or five times before it will need to be recharged by soaking it overnight in a gallon of strong chlorine bleach and then air-drying it in sunlight.

TEST KITS

Pond test kits are available for testing concentrations of ammonia, nitrite, and nitrate, as well as the water's pH. Unless the pond is filled with well water, pH is not usually of concern. Nitrate testing is not critical either as nitrate toxicity is unlikely in the pond, even in the greenest of water. Ammonia and nitrite testing is very important for the well-being of fish.

The most accurate test results are rendered by dry tab tests. A specific amount of pond water is collected in the test tube, to which is added a dry tablet. Once the tablet has dissolved, the water color is compared to a color chart that gives concentrations in parts per million as well as helpful interpretations.

chapter seven

ALGAE

A pond kept free of algae affords the most enjoyment.

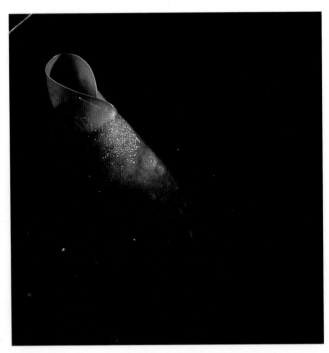

A water lily leaf emerging through filamentous algae is prevented from unfurling at the water's surface.

NATURAL PREVENTION AND REMEDIES

The most effective way to achieve an algae-free pond is by establishing what is commonly called "eco-balance," planting the appropriate number of plants necessary to use the water's nutrients to the exclusion of the lower algae life-form. Submerged aquatics such as elodea, cabomba, sagittaria, hornwort, and ele-ocharis are the primary factor in this equation. Generally, one bunch per square foot of pool surface is recommended. A high fish population mandates an even greater amount of submerged plants to accommodate both the increased bio-load in the pond as well as the "grazing" by fish.

Elodea canadensis is one of the earliest submerged plants to break dormancy in the early spring. Because it may begin showing growth a full month before other such plants, it is possible with the presence of enough *Elodea canadensis* to avoid the usual spring algae bloom. Since the plant takes most of its nutrients directly from the water through its leaves, its roots function primarily to anchor the plant. Consequently, elodea may be potted in only pea gravel to avoid risking spilled soil in the pool. A vigorous grower, it usually requires thinning and control by summer.

If the pool water is already green, it may take as much as six weeks to effect clear water through appropriate amounts of submerged plants. Under green water conditions, submerged aquatics should be moved from the pool bottom to near the water's surface where they will receive the sunlight needed for growth. As the water clears, they may be lowered into a more appropriate depth. Ponds that are lined with two to four inches of pea gravel and carpeted with the "tame" dwarf sagittaria planted directly in the gravel are unlikely to experience any green water algae at all.

The amount of light reaching the pond's surface can be controlled with floating or surface plants. One-third to two-thirds of the water surface should be covered with lily pads or floating aquatics such as water lettuce (*Pistia* sp.), water hyacinth (*Eichhornia* sp.), Fairy moss (*Azolla* sp.), Water velvet (*Salvinia natans*), or duckweed (*Lemna* sp.). Any surplus can be removed. Taller marginal aquatics can be planted along the sunny-side edge of the pool to provide additional shading. Likewise, plants such as miscanthus can be planted at the pond's edge. It is possible to have clear water without surface shading, but this requires a greater number of submerged aquatics to successfully compete for the available nutrients. For example, a pool carpeted with sagittaria would not require as many surface plants for algae-prevention purposes.

Richard Schuck's Ten Percent Solution plant filtration system (described in Chapter Five, "Filtration Alternatives," pages 37–38) effectively uses the principles of eco-balance in controlling green water algae. Similarly, plant basins created in the waterfall may accommodate watercress (*Nasturtium officinale*) or water hyacinth to aid in nutrient removal from the water. Both water hyacinth and water lettuce are good competitors for nutrients in the water.

Avoid topping off the pond often or making frequent water changes with nutrient-rich tap water. Well water may also be high in dissolved mineral salts. Use a test kit to determine the pH, ammonia, nitrite, and nitrate levels of the water being added to the pool. If the added water is nutrient-rich, and especially if pool maintenance routines call for regular water changes, a higher concentration of submerged aquatics will be necessary.

Changing the pool water to eliminate green water algae is but a temporary solution. Besides granting a fresh supply of nutrients to the algae, substantial water changes can stress both plants and fish. Filamentous algae commonly occurs in the clearest of water. However, such algae can be removed manually by twirling a bottle brush or stick in its midst. The implement should be thoroughly washed in bleach and rinsed well

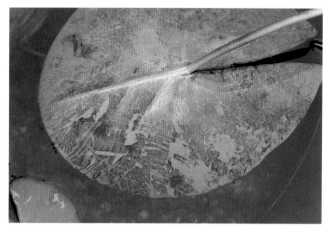

*T*he noxious-smelling blue-green algae can coat the undersides of lily leaves and disrupt their respiration.

after use.

Use caution and follow directions in using liquid plant fertilizers. Too much nutrient will feed algae as well as risk fish. Provide alternate run-off paths or drainage provisions around the pond to avoid the surface entry of fertilizer-enriched water. Likewise, prevent washing in of soil from around the pool. Besides clouding the water, exposed soil is a fresh supply of nutrients.

Use heavy garden soil for potting aquatics. Peat and humus-enriched soils are not necessary for aquatics and only leech nutrients into the water. Line planting containers with hessian, or natural, untreated burlap, to prevent soil leakage into the water. Top all pots with a generous layer of pea gravel. Since some fish, especially koi, like to nose about in the rocks and the soil around plants, a heavier layer of gravel may be required.

Keep the fish population within bounds; fish wastes add nutrients to the water. Feed fish only what they will consume in five minutes. Uneaten food and powdery residues only contribute to the bio-load. If the

*L*ifted into the air, filamentous algae quickly dries and attracts aphids.

pool is well established, there will be natural food sources available. Particularly during the summer months, it may be better to feed the fish small quantities several times a day.

Install small recycling pumps and spouting water features in stagnant areas of the pool that invite algae growth.

Install the waterfall pump at the opposite side of the pool to ensure water circulation and turnover. This is especially important for the good work performed by nitrifying bacteria. While some sources recommend turning over the water once every four hours, factors such as sufficient quantities of submerged plants make this suggestion optional.

Because algae feed on dissolved nutrients in the water, an oxygenating fountain does not ensure clear water. Such oxygenation merely ensures a richer supply for the nitrifying bacteria and fish. Likewise, a biological filtration system may appear to help control green water algae, but in fact the nitrate end-product provides food for the algae. Again, sufficient quantities of submerged aquatics are required to deprive the

The bubbles trapped in scummy patches of floating algae indicate the presence, also, of decomposing organic matter.

algae of this food. The use of a fine filtration media in the bio-filter will remove the tiny green water algae, but frequent cleaning is required to preserve the integrity of the bio-filtration.

Nitrifying bacteria, such as found in biological filters, can be added directly to the pool water. These bacteria require circulating water and the proper pH and temperature ranges. (See Chapter Five, "Inadequate Bio-Filtration," pages 32–35.) Under these conditions, the bacteria may effect a temporary reduction in green water algae. Be sure to have enough submerged plants to utilize the bacteria's nitrate end-product to prevent an algae recurrence.

In established ponds only, freshwater mussels (*Anodonta unio* and *Dreissena* sp.), placed in trays of 3 to 4 inches of sand, will filter free-floating algae from the water at a rate of 10 to 15 gallons per day. The recommended stocking rate is one clam per 20 gallons of water. These mussels may be available from a local market, pet store, or retail aquatic company. Do not use saltwater mussels as they quickly perish, creating an incredible stench and polluted water.

Water fleas (*Daphnia* sp.) will eat free-floating algae. Starter cultures may be purchased from wildlife plant nurseries or fish hatcheries. They should be propagated in water that has been enhanced with straw, crushed aquatic plants, or active yeast, and the container placed in strong, indirect sunlight. Screening may be used to move the daphnia to the pool. Besides assisting in controlling algae, the daphnia are a favorite fish food.

Tadpoles will hide among and feed upon the filamentous and tufty forms of algae. While toad tadpoles will usually spend a short time in the pool, frog tadpoles may be present for two years before metamorphosis into frogs.

Ramshorn, Trapdoor, or Apple snails will feed upon the tufted algae growing on pots or poolsides and on filamentous algae. Occasionally, these species of snails have been known to feed upon aquatic plants; they should be watched closely for such damage. The recommended stocking rate is one snail per square foot of pool surface area. The tall, pointed Great Pond Snail will multiply prolifically and feast upon the aquatic plants; it should be removed.

Grass carp or the white amur will eat only some forms of filamentous algae. Being large fish at maturity, they require large ponds. Also, they eat aquatic plants, so it is best to avoid them altogether. Additionally, they are illegal in much of the United States, and possession of them earns a sizable fine.

*N*utrient-rich water provides favorable growing conditions for many kinds of algae.

The Israeli algae eater (IAE) and koi will eat some forms of filamentous algae. Both fish attain large sizes and should be considered only for ample-sized ponds. The IAE is a prolific breeder and should be incorporated only when bluegill are present as the bluegill emit a hormone that renders the IAE sterile. While their use is best confined to natural earth-bottom ponds, neither fish may be relied upon as a simple solution.

Mesh bags containing granular pond peat release humic acids that reduce algae growth. They should be removed from the pool as soon as decomposition begins to prevent nutrient additions. Silicates or phenolic compounds are produced by barley and wheat straw confined in mesh bags and placed in the pool water. These compounds bind nutrients, thereby starving the green water algae, as well as promoting the growth of algae-eating organisms. The straw should be removed before decomposition can occur. This can be a very effective winter remedy to prevent spring algae blooms.

Salt at a ratio of 2.5 gm/l or 2 lb/100 gal will kill algae. Tannin flocculants coagulate the dying algae for easy removal by skimming or vacuuming.

The mechanical filter attached to a submerged pump should be kept clear of trapped debris, which can decompose into additional algae nutrients. This filter should always be cleaned before restarting a pump that has been inactive for a time as decomposition can occur and add to the pond's bio-load.

The smooth algae growth on pool and pot sides is considered a sign of good health in a pond. Called by some sources a "passive filter," such algae growth aids in removing nutrients from the water which might feed less desirable forms of algae.

Microscopic suspended algae will make the pool water thick and green.

CHEMICAL REMEDIES

Before using chemicals, remove as much algae as possible by hand. Maximum effectiveness occurs above 50°F. The dying algae should always be removed from the water to prevent their decomposition and production of additional nutrients.

Caution should be exercised with the use of chemicals in the pond. Any algicide is likely to slow the growth of higher plant forms, and high dosages may kill them. A way of avoiding strong chemical dosages is to effect a fifty percent water change and then treat the pool with a half dose.

Potassium permanganate, at a concentration of 2 ppm or 2 mg/l, is used to treat green water algae only on cool, cloudy days when the water is not too warm. Sunlight and warm water will cause the treated water to turn a murky yellow. Draining the pool may be avoided by administering another treatment. A maximum of three applications on three successive days is usually recommended. Remove the dead algae when the treatment is concluded.

Formaldehyde, in the common 37 percent solution, may be used at a rate of one drop per gallon of pool water to kill free-floating algae. Since some lily cultivars may also be destroyed, it is best to remove plants from the pool being treated in this way. As this dosage is appropriate for treating fish parasites, it is not necessary to house fish elsewhere during treatment. Avoid skin contact or breathing of this highly toxic chemical.

Particularly in large bodies of water, forms of copper sulfate are commonly used to eradicate algae. Dosages of .33 ppm may be used on alternate days over a two-week period in the presence of fish. If no fish are present, a dosage of 2 ppm may be used. Caution is advised since copper sulfate combines with the fish's body mucus and can cause death by asphyxiation. Copper sulfate, in appropriate dosages, is reputed to be harmless to higher plant forms. Higher pH readings of the water may necessitate a stronger dose. If copper sulfate is used, be prepared to cope with oxygen depletion in the water.

Simazine may be used at a dosage of 0.5 mg/l in small pools before the algae bloom is too great. If used properly, simazine is safe for use with goldfish and koi. Any dosage will affect or kill more sensitive fish such as orfe or rudd, snails, and aquatic plants. All plants should be moved to holding facilities before treatment is begun. Supplemental aeration should be provided as oxygen levels in the pool may be affected for several weeks.

The herbicide urea maleate is considered safe for use with goldfish and koi, but is deadly to more sensitive fish like orfe, as well as to snails and all aquatic plants.

During the early spring, before aquatic plants have attained sufficient growth to successfully compete with the algae for the available nutrients, a non-toxic blue or black aquatic dye may be used to reduce the

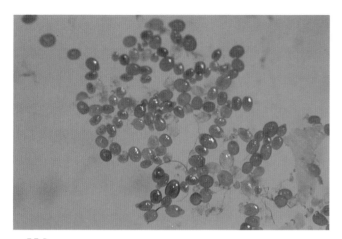

*W*atermeal **(Wolffia** *sp.*), *a tiny floating plant enlarged here, is often confused with algae.*

amount of sunlight entering the pool. Submerged aquatics and water lilies should be moved closer to the pool's surface to access as much sunlight as is possible. The dye is removed later through partial water changes.

Pond Balance, a product presently available only outside the United States, is reported to adjust the water chemistry to make conditions unsuitable for the growth of filamentous algae. The product is reported safe for use in the presence of all pool life. For maximum effectiveness, it may be necessary to use the product repeatedly throughout the season. A full three doses in both spring and autumn is required.

MECHANICAL REMEDIES

Filtration units may be used singly as with Clair Henley's suggestion described in Chapter Five, "Filtration Alternatives," pages 37–38, or as a part of a larger filtration unit in a bio-filter. Such filtration is effective only if the medium is sufficiently dense to trap the microscopic algae. Due to the frequency of cleaning required for such use—sometimes several times a day—the medium should be easily handled; media such as sand or fine gravel are inappropriate. Foam or nylon stockings are easily removed.

Ultraviolet sterilizers may be very effective when used in conjunction with a filtration system. Water flows past the UV light, which kills the algae. The units are usually fitted after the main pond filter to prevent solids from flowing through the unit and lessening the light's penetration into the water. Wattage and flow rate should be matched properly for maximum efficiency. For example, a 1,000-gallon pool would require a 30-watt "inline" sterilizer with the water flowing at a rate of 500 gallons per hour through the unit. In practice, the lamp is turned on when the water begins to appear cloudy. As might be expected, the mechanical filter will require frequent cleaning during the initial clearing period. Any dead algae should be removed from the pool.

Magnetic filters, which are employed within filtration systems, are reputed to limit the availability of nutrients in the water. The effectiveness of such filters has yet to be determined as it appears considerable time is required to effect results.

chapter eight

PLANTS

Although most aquatic plants need a full day of sunlight, some, such as this N. 'Hal Miller,' tolerate less-than-ideal conditions.

Elodea canadensis *can deprive water lilies of needed growing area if it is not thinned and kept under control.*

STOCKING LEVELS

The rationale of suggesting plant stocking levels in the pool is to establish an ecologically sound balance. Generally, this eco-balance is assessed by water clarity and water quality. While an avid water lily hobbyist may indulge in a pool completely covered with lily leaves and a koi hobbyist may rely all but solely on filtration systems, the average water garden will include fish and the three types of aquatic plants—submerged, floating, and marginal.

Submerged plants, deriving much of their nutrients directly from the pool water, are the critical factor in establishing an eco-balance and preventing green water (i.e., algae). As a higher plant form than algae, they will dominate in the removal of mineral nutrients from the water. The general recommendation for stocking submerged aquatics is one bunch per square foot of water surface. Ponds with a high fish population will require greater amounts of plants. A pool that remains green into the summer requires a greater amount to help establish the balance reflected by clear water.

A *sprouting water plantain* (Alisma) *reaches the water surface several inches above the water-clarifying* **Elodea canadensis.**

Elodea canadensis, *left, awakens from dormancy a full month before the commonly available* **Lagarosiphon major,** *right.*

Plants such as water hyacinth (Eichhornia), allowed to multiply without control, can quickly exceed the pond's stocking level.

Generally speaking, larger pools require a less proportionate quantity.

Floating plants such as water hyacinth (*Eichhornia* sp.) and water lettuce (*Pistia* sp.) are characterized by trailing roots that absorb nutrients from the water. Tiny floating plants such as duckweed (*Lemna* sp.), Fairy moss (*Azolla* sp.) and Water velvet (*Salvinia natans*) grow in the same manner. Control over the population of these plants can be maintained by netting out excess plants. Water lilies and plants such as water hawthorne (*Aponogeton* sp.) and floating heart (*Nymphoides* sp.) are grown in soil but send their leaves to float upon the water surface. While the true floating plants assist with nutrient removal, all plants floating on the water surface aid in establishing eco-balance by lessening the amount of sunlight entering the water. Because most submerged aquatics do require sunlight for growth, and because oxygen enters the pool where the water meets the air, it is generally accepted that no

more than sixty percent of the pond's surface be covered with plants.

Marginal and bog plants are, for the most part, simply aesthetic. Roots which escape the pot may help remove nutrients from the water, but they are not a primary factor in establishing eco-balance.

DISINFECTING NEW PLANTS

Introducing plants from the wild is ill-advised since the water garden naturally attracts its own share of pests and parasites. Plants from even the most reputable sources should be disinfected before being placed in the pool. Immerse the plants in a solution of 4 to 6 tablespoons of potassium permanganate crystals to 12 to 13 gallons of water for an hour or two. Foliage only may be bathed for five minutes in a solution of two tablespoons of vinegar to six and one half gallons of water. Bare root water lilies should be soaked several hours or overnight in a Subdue®-type fungicide. Pot-

The roots of even a small water hyacinth (Eichhornia) can be as much as a foot long.

The bloom of the water hyacinth (Eichhornia) appears only in sunny conditions and lasts but a single day.

ted plants should be soaked for two or three days to allow the systemic fungicide to enter the lily's system.

SUBMERGED PLANTS

The roots of most submerged aquatics serve primarily to anchor the plant. Consequently, plants such as elodea or sagittaria may be planted in pots of pea gravel to avoid the risk of spilled soil from tipped pots. They may also be planted directly in pea gravel used to line the pond bottom. If these plants are potted in soil, the pots should be lined with hessian, or natural burlap, and topped with an inch of pea gravel. Because submerged aquatics require sunlight for photosynthesis, they experience better growth in depths of no more than three feet.

Plants such as elodea and parrot's feather (*Myriophyllum* sp.) may be propagated by cuttings. Simply anchor the cuttings in pots of gravel or gravel-topped

soil. Plants such as vallisneria send off side-shoots of growth that may be separated. Hornwort (*Ceratophyllum* sp.) floats free during the growing season. It is simply placed in the water. During the winter, it will anchor itself within a pot on the pool bottom.

Some plants, such as elodea or the curled pondweed (*Potamogeton* sp.), may become aggressive and choke other desired aquatics. The plants can be thinned and the cuttings shared with friends or tossed upon the compost pile. Dwarf sagittaria and vallisneria spread to form a dense "ground cover" that does not interfere with potted aquatics.

Parrot's feather (*Myriophyllum aquaticum* sp.) performs best in less than 12 inches of water. If the growing tip is submerged, it will lengthen to reach the water's surface. Although it is usually potted, pieces that break off will float about the pool and continue to survive. They will eventually anchor in any available pot. New plants may also be started from any shoot along the plant's stem. Since the plant will not survive an icy winter, it should be lowered below the ice level

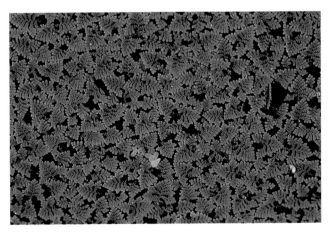

Azolla caroliniana must be kept from blanketing the pond's surface by regularly netting it from the pond.

In repotting pickerel weed *(Pontederia cordata)*, the previous year's rootstock should be trimmed away to prevent rotting.

Duckweed (*Lemna* sp.) seems to spring from nowhere in the early spring. While it limits the amount of sunlight reaching the pond water and in turn discourages algae growth, it can soon attain rampant proportions. The common form, *Lemna minor,* is usually kept under control by the appetites of foraging fish. Larger-sized duckweed does not seem to interest fish and needs to be culled from the pool. Hot summer climates will result in the temporary disappearance of the plant. In ponds where the plant becomes a nuisance, the netting and removal of it during the spring and fall is advisable.

The smallest floating plant is known as water meal (*Wolffia* sp.). This tiny plant appears to be a fine, green grit floating about in the pond's surface waters. Usually lost among other floating plants, it can attain nuisance proportions. If the pool's fish cannot keep it within bounds, a copper or simazine treatment may be required. (See Chapter Seven, "Chemical Remedies," pages 54–55.)

of the pool, where it will winter nicely with a rosy glow about its foliage.

FLOATING PLANTS

Since the planting of a true floating plant involves its simple placement onto the pond's surface, the primary concern is with controlling its natural invasiveness. Too many floating plants may contribute to depletion of oxygen levels overnight. During the heat of summer, particularly in a shallow pool, they may actually trap heat within the pool and help to raise the pool temperature to dangerous levels. Extensive surface coverage during rainy periods or abrupt weather changes results in the upper layer of warmer and oxygenated water mixing with the lower layer of cooler and less oxygenated water ("turning"). This prevents sufficient oxygen exchange at the pool's surface and results in fish stress. Excess plants should be removed from the pool.

Although water mint *(Mentha aquatica)* may be grown in shallow water, its scrambling and unruly growth habit make it better suited for moist planting at the pond's edge.

B*ecause lilies such as "Escarboucle" require substantial surface area, they are not suitable for very small ponds.*

Frogbit (*Hydrocharis* sp.) propagates by sending out side-plantlets that break free to continue multiplying. They will root in shallow pots of marginal plants and create a dense matting about the pot. Excess plants are easily removed by hand. Frogbit reportedly winters over as a small tuber at the pond's bottom, but in reality does not often do this in the lined or concrete pool. Several plants may be brought indoors before the first frost and maintained in a well-lighted container of water. Even so, they generally grow to a smaller and smaller size, seemingly to vanish just short of their return time to the pool.

Azolla is not a favorite fish treat and so may grow unchecked. Colonies of the plant that collect around the shady bases of marginal plants remain green, but extended exposure to direct sunlight results in deep, red-tinged plants. Likewise, as the temperatures cool in the early autumn, the plant turns red. It will survive some frost, but dies over the winter. Unpredictably, it may return in the spring. Excess quantities should be

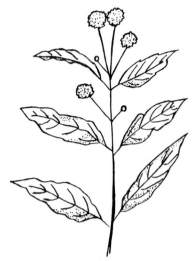

Buttonbush (*Cephalanthus occidentalis*), a native American shrub that may be grown in the informal pond, should be set at water level since the bark contains tannin.

It is possible to winter them over indoors under bright grow-lights in warm water; however, success is uncertain and the cost of operating grow-lights for such a period may prove more expensive than simply replacing the plants the following year.

HARDY WATER LILIES

Hardy water lilies sending up fresh growth in the spring can be helped along by moving their pots into shallow and warmer water of only 4 to 6 inches over the plant's crown. This is especially important in short-summer areas. Once the growth has established and the weather has warmed, the pots can be moved to deeper water.

Water lilies should be planted in mesh or chicken-wire baskets to allow the roots to seek nutrients unobstructed. A solid-walled pot will constrain the lily and reduce its vigor and health. Since chicken wire will sometimes oxidize within one season, care should be exercised in handling, to avoid injury to oneself and the lily. The planting container should be lined with

netted out and tossed upon the compost pile or into the garden, where their fixed nitrogen can be of benefit.

Since the tiny floating plants such as duckweed (*Lemna* sp.), Fairy moss (*Azolla* sp.), or Water velvet (*Salvinia* sp.) grow best as populations, a small portion in the pool may not do well as it disperses about the pool. To protect and encourage the plants' growth, fasten a floatable, plastic loop together and place the small plants within its confines.

Water hyacinth (*Eichhornia* sp.) and water lettuce (*Pistia* sp.) are both tropical plants. They multiply through plantlets sent out on side-shoots. The hyacinth bears a lovely purple bloom that lasts but a day. Water lettuce is a favorite nibbling food of goldfish and koi. Because these plants absorb minerals from the water, they make excellent additions to the compost pile. Excess plants are easily removed from the pool. Occasionally, suspended particulate matter collects on the roots and causes the plants' roots to float to the surface. The plants can be removed from the pool, laid upon the ground, and the roots vigorously hosed clean. By the first frost in temperate climates, the plants should be removed from the pool and discarded.

The invasive common duckweed (Lemna sp.) provides breeding cover and feeding for insect larvae.

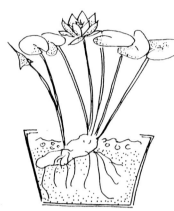

Hardy water lily rhizomes should be planted at a 45° angle with the growing tip at the pot's center.

untreated natural hessian to prevent soil from leeching into the pool water. Burlap will start to rot during a season and may be all but nonexistent by the second season. If a lily is to be left undisturbed for more than one season, a double layer of burlap is merited.

While it is commonly recommended to plant hardy lilies in generous-sized containers, many people find such pots awkward and heavy to manage. Commercially available lily baskets are of a more manageable size and range from the equivalent of a standard mum pot to a 3 or 4 gallon nursery pot. Lilies planted in such pots will usually require repotting each spring.

The pot selected is determined by the lily tuber or cultivar. Tuberosa and odorata tubers are horizontal rhizomes with many "nubbies," or growing eyes, and branches. They require a broader pot to accommodate this growth habit. Marliac tubers tend to be a vertical clump without extensive side-branching. While they may be potted in a less broad container, the larger cultivars require more soil supplied by deeper containers.

The soil used for planting lilies should be of good, heavy garden loam that is free of organic or peat additives. Soil with a proportion of clay proves satisfactory. A handful of bone meal may be mixed into the bottom layer of soil to enhance root development.

Most authorities recommend a slow-acting, low-nitrogen fertilizer at a rate of one ounce or one tab per quart of soil, while others contend a fast-release fertilizer with ammoniacal nitrogen is best. In either case, it is best to add fertilizer after the plant has re-established its root system, which occurs rapidly in hot weather.

Always top the planting with a generous layer of pea gravel. The temptation to use decorative stone should be avoided as it may affect water quality. Flattened type gravel proves more difficult for fish to nudge about. Contrary to popular opinion, goldfish and shubunkin do root in pots searching for delectable larvae. Even if no fish were present, the gravel topping prevents soil from leeching into the pool water and producing turbid conditions.

Extra health insurance is offered plants when the entire pool bottom is covered with a 3- to 6-inch layer of pea gravel. Plant roots grow out into the gravel and derive nutrients from settled particle matter.

Water lily leaves live about three weeks in the summer. The leaves of this "Arc-en-Ciel" display the distinctive rosy coloration of new growth, the cream and green of mature leaves, and the yellowing and decay of dying leaves.

Several distinct growing points, one pushing out of the container's side, are a sign of the need to divide and repot a lily.

A fertile water lily fruit floats free of the coiling stem of its flower.

Indications of the need to repot a water lily are leaves piling upon each other when the lily is set at an appropriate depth with sufficient surface area, a decrease in the usual number of blooms for the cultivar, early yellowing of leaves occurring in less than two weeks in the summer, and a smaller size of mature leaves.

To repot a water lily, the plant is removed from the pot in a shady location. Any leaves should be kept misted to prevent drying. The soil is hosed vigorously from the tuber to fully expose the tuber. Growing eyes, or nubbies, may be noticed along the tuber. These can be popped off by hand or cut off with a sharp knife. Any growing tip may be cut from the tuber with approximately two inches of tuber attached. All exposed cut surfaces of the lily tuber may be dusted with powdered charcoal or an antifungal powder. The rhizome is placed at a 45° angle with the cut end of the tuber placed near the pot's wall to allow for maximum growing room. Damp soil should be tamped firmly about the tuber to prevent its floating from the container. (Even well-tamped dry soil contains enough air

In a short time, the fruit breaks up into individual jelly-wrapped seeds that float for a brief time.

to float the plant free.) The growing tip should remain clear of soil and gravel topping. Wearing thin rubber gloves when working with lily tubers will prevent the roots' blue-black staining the hands.

It is commonly noted that water lilies are heavy feeders. However, fresh soil supplied each year will usually provide sufficient nutrients for healthy growth of the hardy species. If additional feeding is desired, commercially prepared fertilizer tabs are available to be pushed down into the lily's soil at a rate of one tab per quart of soil. Powdered forms of fertilizer may be mixed with mud at a rate of one ounce of fertilizer per rolled ball and then dried for pushing down into the lily's soil. This same amount of fertilizer may also be rolled into a paper napkin for insertion into the soil. Lilies that are into their second year in the same soil should be watched for early yellowing of leaves that may indicate the need for supplemental feeding. An undernourished plant is susceptible to disease or pest attacks.

A water lily blossom lasts four to five days with its summer leaves lasting two to three weeks. Spent blossoms and yellowing leaves should be removed to prevent decomposition in the pond. Besides adding to the pool's bio-load, such decay also invites fungal infections and insect attacks. The dying foliage and blossoms should be pinched off near the plant crown. Yanking or tearing them encourages fungal infections.

If fertile seed has been set, a fruit will form within the flower. The flower stem will coil beneath the

"Helvola," a true pygmy lily, is especially hardy, compliments of an Alaskan **N. tetragona** *parent.*

water's surface, submerging the fruit. After the fruit has ripened, it is loosened from the flower and floats to the surface, where it will shortly break into gel-coated seeds that float there for a brief period. The seeds may be gathered and stored in a container of water. They can also be collected by tying a mesh or nylon bag around the fruit while it is still submerged. Tying plastic bags around the fruit can overheat and destroy the fruit. Many lilies produce fertile seed towards the end of the growing period. The collected seed can be stored over the winter in clean pond water in a cool, non-freezing, dark place. Refrigeration may be necessary to prevent germination. They should be planted in small, shallow containers with but a thin sand coating and allowed to germinate in strong, indirect light, the container submerged in shallow water.

Normally, lily roots that grow out of the container's holes are clean and white. A brown film that is usually noticed on plant labels may also coat the exposed lily roots. This coating is caused by protozoan diatoms that interfere with the lily's attempts to feed. The lily may become weakened and susceptible to infection and insect attacks. The potted lily should be removed from

"Hollandia" is a large, glowing, pink-to-white water lily.

"Solfatare," an apricot-hued beauty, is especially suited to the smaller pond.

the pool and the discolored roots wiped clean. When the plant is returned to the pond, the extended roots should be covered with pea gravel.

Leaves massing and piling upon one another is usually an indication that the lily needs more surface area. If there is enough surface area, the lily may need to be moved to deeper water, the container may be too small for the cultivar, or the plant needs to be divided and repotted.

A soft cloth may be used to gently wipe the stems and undersides of the lily leaves to remove algae growth, sedimentation, and insect eggs. Keeping the undersides of the leaves clean aids in the plant's respiration. Most of the eggs that are wiped from the leaves will be eaten by the fish. Better insect control may be effected by collecting the eggs and disposing of them outside the pool.

Filamentous algae can choke water lilies, stress the plant, and leave it vulnerable to disease or insects. Remove the algae by hand or by twirling a brush or stick.

Keep water lilies at a distance from waterfalls and fountains. They are not happy in moving water, nor do they appreciate water droplets that might burn their leaves in sunny weather.

Occasional strong winds or storms may disrupt water lilies, but new growth allows the plants to recover. Constant exposure to strong winds may exhaust a plant's efforts to survive. Taller marginal plants or tall ornamental grasses on the windward side of the pool may provide the necessary windbreak.

Hailstorms can desecrate a water lily. Extensive hail damage invites fungal infections with the rotting of damaged leaves. All badly affected foliage should be removed to allow the plant to send up new growth. If necessary, all leaves may be removed from the plant, with new growth appearing shortly thereafter.

Occasionally, a lily may produce a mass of tiny leaves at the crown and throughout the pot. This condition is known as fasciation. Little bloom, if any, will be produced due to the reduction in plant vigor. The plant should be removed from the pot and thoroughly hosed clean of soil. Separate the growth and individually replant only the most vigorous of plantlets. The plant may then resume normal growth. If normal growth does not occur, the plant should be discarded.

An aging "Texas Dawn" lily glows amidst its purple-mottled leaves.

*"**C**harles de Meurville" performs well in a large,
sunny pool.*

Not all water lilies are created equal. Some require more sun than others. Some bloom more heavily than others. Some require greater depth than others. And some require more surface area than others. Marliac or clump-type rootstocks perform better in the cooler climates of Great Britain, Canada, and the northern parts of the United States. If a lily is not identified, requirements can be determined by observation.

A lily may be asking for more space or greater depth if its leaves are piling upon one another or if its leaves are produced upon long stems stretching out from the plant. A good-sized tuber that is not blooming in the presence of some shade may require more sunlight. Even though water lilies may still perform in less than ideal conditions, providing ideal conditions ensures maximum performance, enjoyment, and health of the plant. Most water lilies require a full day of sunlight, although lilies grown in very warm climates may require only five or six hours a day. Consult the following chart for appropriate depths of commonly available cultivars. The spread will generally be two to three times the square of the recommended depth.

1

2

3

4

5

6

7

8

REPOTTING A HARDY WATER LILY

1. Hosing soil from the rootstock reveals growing "eyes."
2. Extended growth can be snapped off by hand.
3. Rooted "eyes" close to the main root may be cut free.
4. These divisions will bloom during the current season.
5. Growing "eyes" are potted for the next season.
6. Maximum growing room occurs with the root's cut end placed at the pot's side.
7. Bone meal, well-rotted compost, and fertilizer may be added.
8. Pea gravel topping completes the potting. Preserve the cultivar's name by writing it on both ends of the tag.

RECOMMENDED WATER DEPTHS
FOR HARDY WATER LILIES

6–12 inches

Red

'Elisiana'
'Froebeli'
'James Brydon'
laydekeri 'Fulgens'
laydekeri 'Purpurata'
'Louise'
N. pygmaea 'Rubra'
'Perry's Red Wonder'

Pink

'Firecrest'
laydekeri 'Lilacea'
laydekeri 'Rosea'
'Pink Opal'
'Rose Arey'
'Rose Magnolia'
'Somptuosa'

White

N. candida
'Caroliniana nivea'
'Gonnere'

'Hermine'
N. odorata minor
   (species)
N. tetragona (species)
N. occidentalis

Changeable

'Aurora'
'Graziella'
'Paul Hariot\
   Chrysantha'
'Phoebus'
'Robinsonii'
'Seignourettii'
'Sioux'
'Solfatare'

Yellow

'Charlene Strawn'
N. pygmaea 'Helvola'
'Moorei'

9–18 inches

Red

'Gloriosa'
'James Brydon'
'Lucida'
'Perry's Baby Red'
'Perry's Radiant Red'
'Perry's Red Beauty'
'Perry's Splendid Baby
　Red'
'William Falconer'

Pink

'Amabilis'
'Arc-en-Ciel'
'Caroliniana perfecta'
'Firecrest'
'Helen Fowler'
'Luciana'
'Perry's Cactus Pink'

'Perry's Crinkled Pink'
'Peter Slocum'
'Pink Starlet'
'Rose Arey'
'Tulipiformis'

White

'Albatross'
'Gonnere'
'Venus'

Changeable

'Cherokee'
'Comanche'
'Indiana'
'Sioux'
'Solfatare'

Yellow

'Charlene Strawn'
'Texas Dawn'

9–24 inches

Red

'Atropurpurea'
'Conqueror'
'Escarboucle' ('Aflame')
'Irene Heritage'
'Meteor'
'Newton'
'Perry's Red Blaze'
'Perry's Red Glow'
'Perry's Red Sensation'
'Perry's Super Red'
'Rene Gerard'
'Vesuve'
'William Falconer'

Pink

'American Star'
'Arethusa'
'Eugene de Land'
'Fabiola'
'Mme. Wilfron
   Gonnere'
'Hollandia'
'Mayla'
'Nigel'
'Pearl of the Pool'
'Perry's Pink Beauty'
'Pink Opal'
'Pink Sensation'
'William B. Shaw'

White

'Hal Miller'
N. odorata 'Alba'
'M. Evelyn Stetson'
'Perry's Double White'
'Perry's White Star'
'Perry's White Wonder'
'Queen of Whites'

Yellow

'Gold Medal'
odorata 'Sulphurea'
   Grandiflora
'Sunrise'
'Yellow Sensation'

15—36 inches

Red

'Attraction'
'Charles de Meurville'
'Conqueror'
'Rembrandt'
'Sultan'

Pink

'Amabilis'
'Brackleyi rosea'
'Colossea'
'Darwin'
'Gloire de Temple sur
    Lot'
'Marliacea carnea'
'Marliacea rosea'
'Mrs. Richmond'
'Norma Geyde'
'Perry's Pink'
'Rosy Morn'
'Rosennymphe'
'Turicensis'

White

'Gladstoniana'
N. 'Alba'
N. 'Alba Plenissima'
N. tuberosa
    'Paestlingberg'

Yellow

'Chromatella'
'Col. A. J. Welch'

TROPICAL WATER LILIES

Tropical water lilies have thinner leaves than the hardy varieties. This makes them more susceptible to wind and sun damage, particularly when they are removed from the pool. Since allowing the leaves to air-dry will result in their loss, they should always be kept misted or covered with wet newspapers or thoroughly wet burlap and tended in a sheltered, shady area.

Tropical water lily tubers are oval in shape and may vary in size from as small as a walnut to as large as an egg. They are planted upright in the pot's center, keeping the growing tip free of soil and gravel topping. Because of the small size of the tuber, the smaller mesh containers are quite acceptable.

A potting mixture of good garden soil mixed at a rate of four parts of soil to one part of well-rotted manure will enhance the lily's performance. Adding a handful of bone meal and fertilizer will promote healthy growth. Being more prolific bloomers than the hardy species, tropical lilies should be fertilized each month of the growing season.

Tropical water lilies should not be placed into the

"Choolarp" is a tropical water lily hybridized by Dr. Slearmlarp Wasuwat of Pang-U-Bon, Thailand.

"Jongkolnee" is another beautiful tropical hybrid of Dr. Slearmlarp Wasuwat of Thailand.

The growing tip of tropical water lilies should be kept free of soil and gravel topping.

pool until the water temperature has stabilized at 70°F. Once their growth has become established, they will survive fluctuations in temperature below this level, as well as survive well into the cooling temperatures of autumn. Viviparous day-bloomers and the blue varieties are the hardiest and are better survivors in climates of inconsistent summer temperatures.

Tropical lilies perform best in shallow water depths

of only 6 to 12 inches over the plant's crown. They produce viable seed more often than the hardy varieties. It is not uncommon to find tropical seedlings sprouting from shallow submerged pots of marginal plants. In colder climates it is possible to find that some seed has wintered over in marginal pots and sprouted the following year.

In warm weather climates, tropical lilies may remain in the pool year round. They may experience a brief period of dormancy during a period of cool nights, but will resume growth as the weather warms. Heating the pool to 72°F during such cool periods will prevent the plant from entering dormancy. Likewise, protecting the pond with clear plastic allows wintering over in a fully foliated condition, albeit somewhat reduced in size.

CROWN ROT

Water lily crown rot is more prevalent today than it has been in the past. It is characterized by the leaf and flower stems becoming soft and blackened near the crown and then progressively upwards. Frequently, an early sign is the rotting of a flower bud before it reaches the water's surface. Pulling back the gravel covering of the pot may reveal the roots becoming gelatinous with a rank odor. Because this foul smell precedes the rotting of the tuber itself, it is helpful to be familiar with the normal odor of the lily tuber. As the disease progresses, the plant loses vigor and produces fewer leaves, which turn yellow within the first few days of reaching the surface. Crown rot is a highly contagious fungal infection that can destroy an entire collection of lilies.

Water lilies with dark or mottled foliage, especially yellow cultivars, seem to be the most susceptible to infection. A survey study of crown rot conducted in

1989 by the Ministry of Agriculture, Fisheries and Food in Great Britain noted the hardy lilies 'Attraction' and 'Chromatella' as the most badly and frequently infected. In the United States, the pygmy 'Helvola' seems to be particularly susceptible, as are 'Indiana,' 'Comanche,' 'Sioux,' 'Chrysantha,' and 'Robinsonii.' Lilies reported in the British study as not

The fully double, cup-shaped blooms of the night-blooming, tropical "Bissetii" glow a rosy-pink.

"Trail Blazer," a fragrant, stellate, tropical day-bloomer, was hybridized by Martin Randig in 1938.

*T*ropical water lilies flourish beautifully under glass
in this water lily pool of the Atagawa Tropical
& Alligator Garden in Japan.

affected by crown rot were 'Brackley Rosea,' 'Col. A. J. Welch,' 'Elisiana,' 'Marliacea Rosea,' 'Rembrandt,' 'Rene Gerard,' 'Seignourettii,' and 'William B. Shaw.'

Because a plant may appear healthy for a time before showing signs of infection, it is wise to treat all incoming lilies as though they are infected. A holding tank for new lilies should be set up; if the lily is bare-rooted, a bucket will suffice. The lily tuber should be soaked in a solution of five drops of the oily Subdue®fungicide per gallon of water for a period of several hours.

Soaking overnight will not harm the tuber. Potted lilies should be left in this solution for two or three days to allow the systemic fungicide to be fully absorbed into the plant's system. Simply dipping the tuber or plant in the solution will not afford protection. Other fungicides of powder form which have been used with some effectiveness are Aaterra, Basilex, Benlate®, Filex, Fungex®, Sulphur and Truban®.

A plant that is obviously infected should be removed from the pool and kept away from all other

Crown rot, a highly contagious fungal infection, can rapidly spread and destroy an entire lily collection.

plants. Vigorously hose off soil to allow observation of the tuber. If unaffected growth shoots are present on the tuber, they should be cut off and soaked in the fungicide solution before repotting. The new plant should be kept quarantined until it is certain the plant is free of the fungal infection.

All water lilies in a pool in which crown rot has been detected should be treated appropriately with fungicide. If no fish are present in the water, copper sulfate may be used as a preventive measure. Place copper sulfate crystals in a nylon or muslin bag and drag through the pool water until they are fully dissolved.

The best safeguard against crown rot is good pool hygiene and preventing stress to the lilies. Stressful conditions such as transportation, removal from water, repotting and division, drastic water temperature changes such as adding cold water to a warmed pool, lack of feeding or repotting when nutrition has been exhausted from the soil, and lack of sufficient sunlight may render a lily more susceptible to infection if the pathogen is present.

LEAF SPOTS

Decaying leaf spots on water lily leaves are usually of fungal origin. Another related fungal infection affects the leaves by turning them dry and brown about the edges. Both conditions will occur during humid or prolonged rainy periods. Exposing the leaves to drastic changes in water temperature or insect attacks may also produce injured areas on the leaves that invite the fungal infection. All affected leaves should be removed from the plant and destroyed. Even if all leaves must be removed, new growth will soon replace them.

A weak solution of Bordeaux may be sprayed onto the leaves. Because this solution can harm fish, the treatment should be effected in a separate treatment tub for a few hours or overnight. Fungicides such as those listed for the treatment of crown rot may also be effective in such isolated treatments.

LEAF MINERS

Several insects, such as the leaf mining midge (*Chironomus* sp.) will lay eggs that hatch into minute, tunnelling larvae that meander through the water lily leaf leaving a delicate trail that rots through in ragged and disfigured patterns. A heavy infestation will produce skeletonized leaves. Dwarf and pygmy cultivars can become weakened and die from the attack. Affected leaves should be removed and destroyed.

Infested plants can be moved to a treatment tub for a bath in nicotine or malathion. *Bacillus thuringiensis,* which parasitizes the larvae, may also be effective. The bacillus is available in powder form and is mixed with water and sprayed onto the affected leaf. Applying bacteria in powder form is messy and unsightly. If the leaves are sprayed within the pool, avoid heavy spraying and confine the spray to the affected leaves. B.t. is naturally more effective in treating the surface-tunnelling *Cricotopus* sp., the false leaf mining midge, since the bacteria can more easily come into contact with the larvae. Since the eggs of these insects are usually laid upon the leaf's surface, a preventive hosing of the leaves may knock the eggs into the water for consumption by fish.

APHIDS

Aphids attacking water lilies and other succulent aquatics such as water plantain (*Alisma* sp.), Arrowhead (*Sagittaria* sp.), bog bean (*Menyanthes* sp.), or pickerel rush (*Pontederia* sp.) may be black, green, or white in color. Feeding upon the leaves and flowers, the aphids reduce the plant's vigor and can kill it.

Mild infestations are said to be controlled by vigorously hosing the insects from the plant into the water where they are consumed by fish. However, in practice, it often appears the insects are agile enough to scramble back upon the plant before the fish notice the frantic activity. The fish most likely to notice their flounderings is the orfe, which schools at the water surface seeking such delicacies.

Insecticides may be used if the affected plants are moved to a separate treatment facility. Pyrethrum, nicotine soap, or derris solution may be effective. These treatments are toxic to fish and should never be used in their presence.

A light spray of vegetable oil may smother the insects. Good pool hygiene and proper care of the plants is the most effective preventive measure. Aphids are attracted to undernourished and weakened plants. Since aphids over-winter in flowering plum and cherry trees, the trees should be sprayed with an oil wash in the late autumn.

CADDIS FLIES AND MOTHS

Caddis flies are found in all parts of the world. Their eggs are laid under water, where the larvae hatch to build shelters of debris on the pool bottom where they roam about feeding upon plant roots and stems. A regular routine of vacuuming debris from the pool bottom will prevent their damage.

Most resource books mention the China mark moth as a pest of water lilies. This moth is still primarily confined to the European continent and has been reported thus far only in the far eastern United States. However, as aquatic plants are shipped from one place to another, it may be but a matter of time before this moth makes its presence widely known. Nevertheless, other moth species abound in all parts of the world, their behavior and habits quite similar to those of the China mark moth. Moths visit the pool in the evening hours and lay eggs in neat rows on the undersides of lily leaves. These eggs hatch in 10 to 14 days. The tiny larvae build shelters of pieces of leaves and debris on the water's surface. Safely hidden in their shelters, the larvae float about the pool feasting on whatever greens they encounter. A regular maintenance routine of softly wiping the leaf undersides will dislodge the eggs for fish consumption. Any floating debris in the pool should be netted out and disposed of away from the pool area.

Other moth larvae, caterpillars, will eat holes in lily leaves and burrow into the plant's stems. *Bacillus thuringiensis* may be an effective control if it can be sprayed directly on the caterpillars or where they are feeding. Any insecticides that are used should be applied in a separate treatment tank fully away from the pond.

LEAF BEETLES

If the pool is located near a natural body of water, leaf beetles (*Chrysomelidae, Donaciinae*) may find their way to the pool. Their eggs are laid in neat rows on the undersides of water lily leaves or on the submerged stems of marginal plants. The robust, grub-like larvae may be unnoticed among thick masses of leaves where they feed upon the foliage beneath the water's surface. They are more usually found about the roots of aquatic plants. During late-season repotting, silky-cased pupae may also be found affixed to the lily tuber.

The best method of control is to practice a regular routine of wiping the eggs from the leaves. A gentle rub with the thumb will loosen them from the leaves if collection and disposal are desired. Since the larvae eventually end up feeding about the roots of aquatic plants, control can be difficult. A severe infestation may merit removing the plant from the pool to thoroughly hose the soil and larvae from the plant and then repot in fresh, clean soil.

LOTUS

Bare-rooted lotus tubers are available only in the early spring. While they may be dug up, cut back, and planted later in the season, there is less assurance of success.

Lotus tubers are vigorous growers that send out extensive banana-shaped roots with intermittent growing tips. If these tender tips are broken, the plant will perish. Consequently, they should never be planted in square pots. A circular pot allows the roots to grow unimpeded, although the plant is likely to become pot-bound within the course of one season. Most lotus require as large a pot as is manageable. Because the lotus plant can easily grow to five feet in height, they are best suited to a larger pool. Dwarf varieties have been developed that do not require so large a container or pond.

Using a damp soil mixture of two parts garden soil to one part composted cow manure enriched with ample bone meal and 8 ounces of fertilizer, the pot is filled to within 3–4 inches of the gravel-topping level. Tamp the soil firmly to prevent air bubbles from lifting the planted tuber from the pot. Gently lay the tuber in the pot and fill around and over it with a couple more inches of soil. Take care to leave the growing tips free of soil. Because the lotus tuber is planted so shallowly and has no roots to anchor it in the pot, it is imperative that the soil be moistened. After tamping this soil about the tuber, add pea gravel, again avoiding the growing tips. Set the planted container in very shallow water until the root growth has developed enough to hold the plant within the container. It can then be moved into as much as 12 inches of water over the plant's crown.

Because of its vigor, lotus should be fed at least once a month with 8 ounces of low-nitrogen fertilizer. Some plants may require feeding every two weeks. Full sun and a temperature range of 75 to 90°F are necessary

"Momo Botan" is a dwarf lotus suited to the smaller pond or tub planting.

***T**he lotus seed pod can be dried for preserved floral arrangements.*

for blooming. Cooler northern climates of less direct sunlight may not be suitable for satisfactory performance.

Even in warmer climates, the lotus will still experience a brief period of dormancy over the winter months. Repotting is required each spring to accommodate the tuber's extensive growth. The tuber is gently hosed free of soil with special care taken not to injure the brittle growing tips. The tuber may then be cut into pieces of at least one growing tip and one full section of tuber. Dip the cut end in powdered charcoal or a fungicide to help prevent rotting. Pot each section as described above.

LOTUS PESTS

The black aphid (*Rhopalosiphum nymphaeae*) is a rapid multiplier that can quickly cover the entire plant, as can other members of the family. If the infestation is light, a strong hosing will knock the aphids into the pool water for fish consumption. Heavier infestations may require removing the lotus from the pool.

The European cornborer (*Ostrinia nubilalis*) is a common pest that will initially hide within a rolled edge of a leaf. Later, it will burrow into the lotus stem, where it is all but impossible to control. During the initial phase of infestation, the pest can be controlled by hand-picking. Perry B. Slocum, renowned lotus hybridizer, suggests a house and garden push-button bomb sprayer may dislodge them as well, but care must be taken not to spray the pool with such force. Removing the plant from the pool and treating with malathion may also be effective.

Yellow, white, brown, or red fuzzy caterpillars (*Diacrisia virginica*) may attack the lotus in mid- to late summer. If hand control proves ineffective, forceful spraying or isolated malathion treatment may be required.

***L**ike the water lily, the lotus blossom lasts but a few days.*

The beauty of marginal plantings in a shallow pond area is diminished by the rampant growth of water clover (**Marsilea** *sp.*).

MARGINALS

Most marginal aquatics are vigorous growers that require annual repotting. Repotting and division should be performed in the early spring, although it may be performed until mid- to even late summer. Fall division may not give the plant enough time to establish itself before winter dormancy. If the pot is too full of growth to remove the compacted root ball, spray a strong force of water down the inner edge of the pot. It may be necessary to use a knife to cut away the pot.

Thoroughly hose off the soil from the plant's roots. Although the root structure may vary, the principle of including a good portion of root with each growing point should be followed. Cut back the top growth if the root system is too small to feed it. For vigorous growers, a wider-mouthed mum-type container should be used. Line the pot with natural hessian, or untreated burlap, to prevent soil from leeching into the pool. Use good, heavy, garden soil mixed with a handful of bone meal. Avoid humus-enriched soils.

Situate the plant in the pot to allow for maximum

Loosestrife *(Lythrum)*, a fully hardy wildflower species, growing to 4 feet, is a splendid summer bloomer in shallow water, but may reseed freely.

Reed grass *(Phragmites communis)*, effective only in mass planting, is highly invasive. Because it can grow to 12 feet, it is not suited to potting and the small-pool habitat.

unrestricted growth and tamp dampened soil firmly about the roots. Keep growing points free of soil. Top with a generous layer of pea gravel.

Most marginal aquatics are happiest in 2 to 4 inches of water over the plant's crown. Taller aquatics such as cattails and rushes may be grown in deeper water.

Particularly if the plant has been divided and repotted in fresh soil, supplemental feeding is not required during the growing season. However, if the plant has been in the same soil for more than one season, two ounces of low-nitrogen fertilizer may be added monthly per quart of soil.

Wintering the hardy perennial forms of these plants may require no special care at all. If the plant enters a dormancy period, its top should be cut back above the water level in the late fall to prevent the harboring of insect pests as well as possible decomposition in the pond water.

SEMI-HARDY PLANTS

Arrowhead (*Sagittaria* sp.) may be as much as a full month behind other hardy marginals in breaking dormancy in the spring. If it has not resumed growth after that period, remove the plant from the pool and hose the soil from the roots. Viable tubers or root portions may be found. Repot them and discard the rotted portions.

Some species of both arrowhead and pickerel weed (*Pontederia* sp.) may be only marginally hardy. To be certain of saving the plant, lower it below the ice level for the winter. Most species of umbrella grass (*Cyperus* sp.) are not fully hardy. They may be lowered below the anticipated ice level or wintered indoors as a house plant. Always bring such plants indoors before the first frost has induced irreversible dormancy or dying. Removing any seed heads may also aid the plant's survival.

The late-summer-blooming swamp hibiscus is a woody shrub suitable for the informal pond.

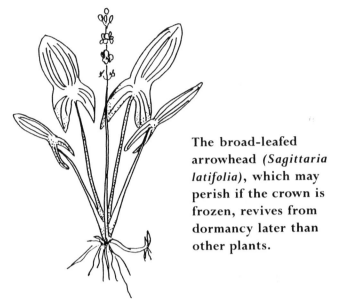

The broad-leafed arrowhead *(Sagittaria latifolia)*, which may perish if the crown is frozen, revives from dormancy later than other plants.

The cardinal flower *(Lobelia cardinalis)* may need to spend its winters in a cold-frame, but its summer attraction in the pond is a hummingbird's delight.

In spite of some reports of the cardinal flower (*Lobelia cardinalis*) surviving a Zone 5 winter, the plant should be removed from the pool before the first frost and the pot buried in soil to its rim in a cold frame for the winter.

MID-SUMMER DORMANT PLANTS

Marsh marigolds (*Caltha palustris*) make a bright, cheerful display in the early spring. By summer, however, they appear to die. If it is not practical to set them inconspicuously in the pool, they may be removed and the pots buried to their rims in the garden, where they can be kept watered until growth resumes.

Water hawthorne (*Aponogeton*) also experiences a mid-summer dormancy. This plant should be left in the pool as it will bloom in both spring and late fall.

The scrambling habit of the bog bean (Menyanthes trifolia) is best suited to the informal pool.

The water forget-me-not (Myosotis palustris) requires a large pot for its most effective showing.

The marsh marigold *(Caltha palustris)* blooms brightly in the early spring and then disappears in summer dormancy.

The dwarf cattail (Typha minima) will grow to four feet, but is unlikely to tip over its pot.

The common cattail (*Typha latifolia*) is impossible to confine to a single pot for even one season. Quickly becoming top-heavy, it will easily tip over.

The tropical and semi-tropical umbrella palm (Cyperus sp.) is available in both dwarf and standard sizes.

The native American blue flag iris (Iris versicolor) rarely exceeds two feet, which makes it a stately choice for the small pond.

The variegated cattail (Typha latifolia var.) is not as invasive or as tall-growing as its common green counterpart.

Horsetail (*Equisetum* sp.) lends a tropical bamboo-like effect to the cold-climate pond.

The semi-hardy species of water canna (Thalia dealbata) *lacks the lush bloom of its tropical relatives.*

Water pennywort (Hydrocotyle verticillata) *is a charming little plant that must be kept within bounds.*

*B*ulrush (Scirpus) *is most effective in a large clump.*

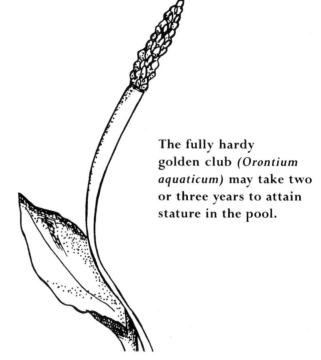

The fully hardy golden club *(Orontium aquaticum)* may take two or three years to attain stature in the pool.

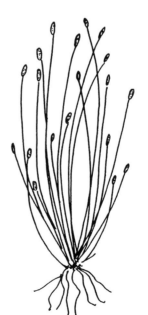

Spikerush (*Eleocharis* sp.), reseeding prolifically, sprouts weedlike in any available pot. Very sensitive to transplanting, it may go into shock for a few days.

REPOTTING CATTAILS

1. A pot-bound plant may have to be cut free of its container.
2. Micro-miniature cattail roots grow around the pot's perimeter.
3. A strong hosing in the center allows access to the plant's roots.
4. Grasp the plant firmly and pull it apart.
5. Well-rooted clumps are pulled from the root mass.
6. Each clump will fill a pot by next season.
7. Larger-sized cattails grow in the same way.

1

2

3

4

5

6

7

REPOTTING RUSHES

1. Scirpus plants grow in tight clumps.
2. Hose the soil from the clump and remove the excess roots. A sharp knife cuts the rooted plant mass into smaller portions.
3. Plant each portion in a separate pot.

1

2

3

REPOTTING PICKEREL WEED

1. Pickerel weed (*Pontederia* sp.) pushes out the sides of a pot and escapes through the pot's bottom holes, often within one growing season.
2. The thick rootstock grows from the previous season's roots.
3. Cut away the old roots and retain viable roots with each plant.
4. Repot in fresh soil, the growing tip directed to the pot's center, and tamp the soil firmly to prevent the plant from floating free. Top with pea gravel.

1

2

3

4

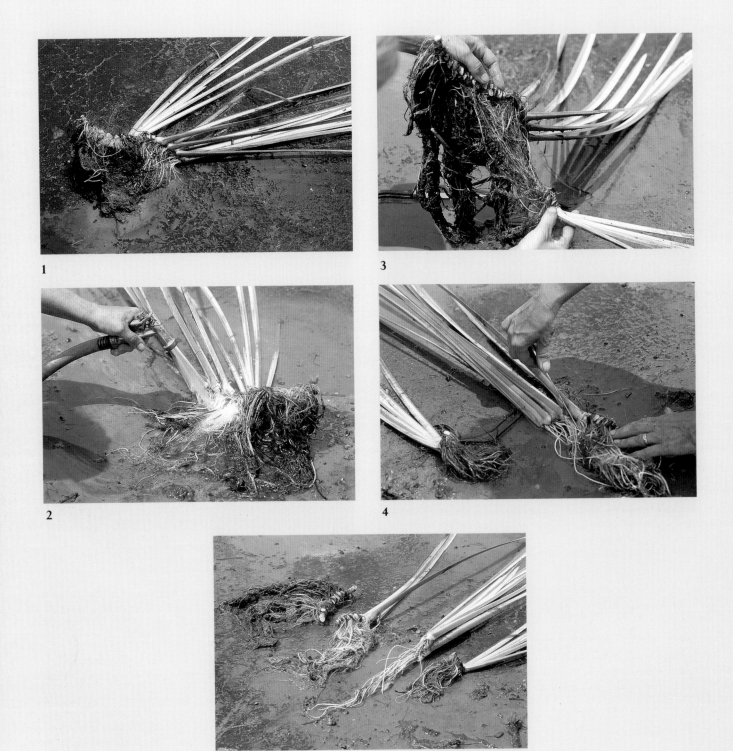

1

2

3

4

5

6

7

REPOTTING SWEET FLAG

1. Sweet flag (*Acorus* sp.) grows from a lengthening rootstock.
2. Hose soil from the roots.
3. Pull larger plants free.
4. Cut rooted, smaller plants from the main root.
5. Each division will be potted separately.

6. Cover the pot's holes with burlap to prevent soil from escaping into the water. Pot the plant to allow maximum growing space.
7. Tamp the soil firmly about the plant's roots, and cover it with pea gravel to prevent leeching.

ATYPICAL PLANTS IN THE POND

Japanese iris (*Iris kaempferi,* now classified as *Iris ensata*) may be grown in the pool during the growing season. It will adjust to one to three inches of water depth over the plant's crown. During the fall, the pots should be buried to their rim in the garden to prevent the roots from rotting.

Siberian iris and ribbon grass (*Phalaris 'picta'*) may be grown in two to four inches of water over the crown year round.

The Arum lily (*Zanteschia aethiopia*) will survive frost if the crown is at least six inches below the water surface. In very cold regions, it is best to remove the plant and store the bulb in damp sand over the winter.

Any moisture-loving plant such as the Royal fern (*Osmunda regalis*), day lilies (*Hemerocallis* sp.), hosta, and astilbe may be placed in the pool during the growing season so long as the plant's crown remains above the water level. Remove the pots in the fall and bury to their rims in the garden.

"*D*irector G.T. Moore" is a tropical shade-tolerant lily.

The royal fern (*Osmunda regalis*), which grows to 3 to 4 feet, does well in the shallow waters of the shadier pool.

ELEVATING PLANTS

Bricks may be stacked to form pedestals on which to place pots. If the pool is lined, a scrap piece of liner between the bricks and liner will help prevent punctures. Concrete blocks, being larger than bricks, require fewer trips to construct a plant pedestal. Rinse the blocks well or paint with a non-toxic sealant to prevent lime from leeching into the pool water. Placing inappropriately treated concrete blocks into the pool can be disastrous for the fish. Use a scrap piece of liner for puncture protection.

Plastic milk crates make a lightweight and stable plant pedestal. While it may be tempting to use half a large 55-gallon plastic drum as a plant pedestal, in practice they are difficult to keep from floating up to the water's surface.

*The pond sited in a shady area will produce lush
foliage, but few, if any, flowers.*

PARTIAL-SUN WATER GARDEN

As a general rule, flowering plants require full sun. In very hot summer climates of direct sun, five to six hours a day may be sufficient. However, ponds in northern climates and ponds that receive only three to five hours of sunlight daily will do better if planted with shade-tolerant plants.

Hardy water lilies that will perform with only three to five hours of direct sun are 'Hal Miller,' 'Masaniello,' 'Chromatella,' 'Attraction,' 'Escarboucle,' 'Froebeli,' 'Comanche,' 'Paul Hariot' and 'Chrysantha.' Shade-tolerant tropical water lilies are 'Director George T. Moore,' a deep purple, and 'Isabelle Pring,' a globular white. Blue varieties, in general, tend to be more tolerant of less-than-ideal conditions.

Submerged plants that perform well under less sunny conditions are parrot's feather (*Myriophyllum* sp.) and hardy cabomba. Water hyacinth (*Eichhornia* sp.) will not bloom. Water lettuce (*Pistia* sp.), having no flower, is fine in partial-sun gardens. Any marginal or bog plant that does not produce flowers will perform well in shade.

*T*he vivid red of "Escarboucle" glows in a
semi-shaded pool.

KOI IN THE WATER GARDEN

Koi have special environmental needs and are, therefore, not suited for life in the water garden. They can be included if the pond is large and deep enough and the koi population kept small. Even though koi may be fed sufficiently, they still require fresh greens in their diet. The pool's submerged grasses and tender submerged lily growth often prove irresistible. Trying to curtail their appetite with daily feedings of fresh lettuce and celery leaves may be for naught; the water garden is a virtual smorgasbord to a koi. It may prove worthwhile to culture small pots of leaf lettuce, cover the soil with flat rocks to prevent nudging about, and set them in the pool for the koi's pleasure.

Cone-shaped netting that extends from the water lily pot to surface floats will prevent the koi from feasting upon lily growth. The biggest argument for not using this protection is that koi do enjoy basking beneath the shelter of lily leaves on hot summer days.

Submerged aquatics can be protected by planting them in trays that are enclosed by a plastic or fiberglass screen box. The box can be left open where it sits on the pool bottom. Plants such as elodea will grow through the screen, allowing the koi to feed only upon what extends beyond the screen. Plants such as dwarf sagittaria and vallisneria will be totally protected.

Unprotected plants should be topped with flat rocks that are more difficult for the koi to nose about the pot. Koi do enjoy rooting in the gravel for fun as much as for seeking insect larvae. An extra generous layer of gravel will prevent them from "unpotting" a freshly potted plant. If the koi seem especially playful, Ping-Pong balls can be floated in the pool or threaded onto fishing line and anchored on the pond bottom.

Plants may be severely damaged during spawning but will usually recover quickly. Damage to plants will be less noticeable if there is an abundance of them. However, if minor skirmishes between plants and koi escalate into all-out war, the water lilies may have to be moved to another pond. Marginal aquatics and lotus are the only options remaining.

chapter nine

FISH

*Enjoyable to watch, fish are necessary in the
garden pond to control mosquito larvae.*

STOCKING LEVEL

In stocking a new pond, the usual recommendation is for no more than one inch of fish per square foot of pool surface area. Established pools may have a maximum stocking level of 2–3 inches per square foot of pool surface area. The water quality of well-stocked pools should always be closely monitored.

FISH SELECTION

The common goldfish, comet goldfish, and shubunkin are the hardiest choices for a water garden. Fancy goldfish such as fantails, moors, orandas, and lionheads are not as hardy and are more easily preyed upon. Orfe require a larger pool and should be kept in a group as they are a schooling fish. Being a more sensitive fish, the orfe should never be exposed to chemicals in the pool water.

Koi require at least 3 feet of depth, a larger-sized pool, and excellent water quality. Lovers of fresh greens, they are not usually suitable for the well-

Colorful calico fantail fish can be a delightful pond addition, but will require extra care and consideration.

The hybrid butterfly koi are graceful pets for the larger pond.

Shubunkin are a colorful and hardy choice for the water garden.

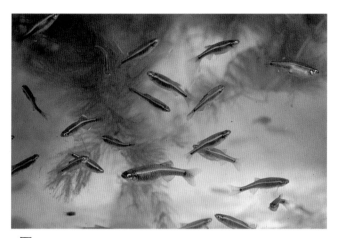

Tiny White Clouds offer colorful mosquito control in warmer climates such as northern Australia.

The Mogurnda adspersa *is commonly used in Australia for mosquito control.*

planted water garden. In warmer climates, the small White Cloud fish is quite adept at mosquito patrol.

The introduction of native fish is generally unwise as the water garden is not environmentally suited to them. The temptation to introduce catfish as scavengers should be avoided as catfish attain good size and will stir up sediment collected on the pool bottom. Also, as they mature, they become predators of small fish.

The aquarium *Plecostomus* species may be introduced as a scavenger and algae eater in warm weather pools only. In temperate zones they should be treated as a tropical fish.

PURCHASING FISH

Bringing home sick or infected fish endangers the existing pool inhabitants and creates a sad, stressful, and expensive situation as the fish become ill, are treated, and perhaps die. Purchase fish only from a reputable dealer.

Talk to the vendor. Does the seller know the basics of common fish diseases and infestations? Can the vendor describe symptoms of these problems? Does the vendor regularly employ preventive treatments of health problems? Does the vendor use a Stress Coat product in the bag with the newly purchased fish?

Observe the fish. Clamped fins, hovering in a corner or at the bottom of the aquarium tank, being nudged by other fish in the tank, ease of catching the fish (little fear of being handled), any abnormal blotching or marking of the fish's body, or ragged state of fins or tail may indicate health problems with the fish. A healthy fish is active and sociable with its kind.

Carefully observe other fish in the tank. Many diseases and infestations are contagious. If one other fish in the tank appears ill, do not buy any fish from the tank.

Do not purchase fish that have recently been brought into the store. Allow time for the transportation shock to disappear in order to ascertain that behavior aberrations are not due to disease. Allow time for the shop to provide preventive treatment for parasites. Even though the fish might initially be healthy, the stress from transportation may make it susceptible to free-swimming parasites that might be in the water. Such infestations will not appear for 10 to 14 days.

Since most parasitic life cycles evolve in 10 to 14 days at pet shop aquarium temperatures, such a waiting period would be ideal. Many pet shops guarantee fish for only twenty-four hours. Other shops guarantee fish for only a week, which is still less than the parasitic life cycle.

Do not add the water in which the fish is transported to the pool or aquarium since it may harbor the free-swimming stage of parasites. Once the water in the floating bag has been equalized with the pool water, transfer the fish by hand. If the fish are being placed directly into the pool, they should be dipped for 10 to 15 seconds in a salt dip of one pound of non-iodized salt per gallon of water.

For the sake of the fish already in the pond, new fish should be quarantined for two weeks in a hospital tank that has one to two tablespoons of non-iodized salt per five gallons of water dissolved in it. A broad-spectrum parasiticide may be used as well. If a quarantine is not possible, the entire pool may be treated with a broad-spectrum parasiticide every three days for three treatments.

STRESS

A fish's health is directly related to its environment. Any change in the fish's environment can produce stress that inhibits the fish's immune system and makes the fish susceptible to diseases, infections, or parasites that may normally be present in the water.

Signs of stress in fish are frantic jumping and swimming, hiding, clamped fins, blushing fins, and red body veining. Commercial Stress Coat products help relieve stress by replacing the fish's natural slime coat, which is shed during stressful experiences. This slime coat helps protect the fish from attacks by parasites. Stress additives also help prevent the loss of cellular fluids and electrolytes. The general dosage is one teaspoon per ten to twenty gallons of water. This treatment can be added to the transport bag, the quarantine tank, or the pool.

Salt at a rate of 2.5 g/l or 2 pounds per 100 gallons acts as both a stress reliever and a general tonic. In treating the entire pool, the pool's volume should be computed in gallons and then divided by 100. Multiply this figure by two pounds to determine the dosage to be used in each of two treatments at a three-day interval. The salt should be dissolved in a large bucket and distributed about the pool. Avoid dumping the saltwater on plants.

Another stress treatment is to dissolve one 50-gram tablet of aspirin in ten gallons of water.

HANDLING OR TRANSPORTATION

Transporting fish from the pet store to the pool is usually accomplished with the fish enclosed in a plastic bag of water inflated with pure oxygen. If the fish are to be transported some distance, advise the proprietor so that extra care may be taken. Likewise, transporting fish in a bucket of water may require a battery-operated air pump for lengthy trips. Without such aeration, the water should be aerated by hand-splashing every half hour.

It is best to keep the fish as dark and cool as possible. Professional fish shippers place the bagged fish in a closed Styrofoam box with a frozen pack beneath the bag. Keeping the water well-chilled during longer trips slows the fish's metabolism, awareness, and need for oxygen.

Placing the fish into a water temperature of but a few degrees' difference can be disastrous. The plastic bag should be floated in the pool for at least 10 to 15 minutes to equalize the two water temperatures. A small bit of pool water may then be added to the bag for another 10 to 15 minutes. The "floating" time will be longer if the fish have been transported with ice. If the seller did not place a stress treatment in the bag, it should be added during the floating process. Likewise, adding a teaspoon of dissolved salt during this process may help to alleviate stress. If the fish is being floated in the bag on a sunny day, place a small towel over the bag to protect it from the strong sunlight.

Lift the fish gently by hand from the bag to his new quarters. Larger fish should be guided by a net into containers. It is better to handle them with gloved hands rather than risking injuries by netting them. If the fish is being added directly to the pool, it may be wise to plunge him for a 15-second dip in a solution of one pound of salt to one gallon of water. This will lessen the possibility of introducing parasites into the pool with the fish.

If the fish is being added from a bucket, keep the bucket covered with a towel or screen to protect the fish from sunlight and to keep him from jumping out. Pool water is added a few cupfuls at a time over a period of time to provide the necessary gradual adjustment of temperatures. A stress coat or bit of salt as described above should be added to assist the fish in dealing with the stress.

Avoid transporting fish when the water temperature is above 90°F since fish are less able to manage stress in this temperature range.

Koi especially are known for jumping from the water when placed in an unfamiliar environment, but a goldfish will do the same. Whether the new fish is placed in a quarantine tank or the pool, observation for the first couple of hours assures that the fish is adjusting to its new quarters. Placing a screen or net over the tank or the pool will prevent a fish being out of water. Be sure there are no gaps large enough for the fish to jump through. Usually a new fish hovers about the bottom of the tank as it recovers from its travels. It is not uncommon for such a supposedly calm fish to be discovered dead outside the tank in the morning.

Feed fish sparingly the first few days to allow for recovery from transport shock. If a net is used, thoroughly disinfect it between uses.

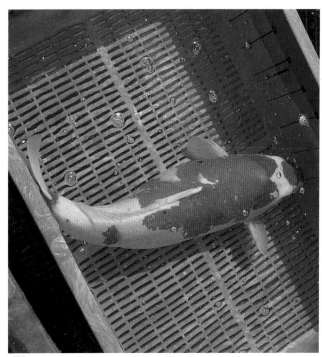

This Mag Noy Kohaku displays the desirable snow-white body with well-defined **hi,** *or red markings.*

*K*oi are bred to be viewed from above. This Mag Noy Taisho Sanke (tricolor) is a strking pond pet.

*O*fer Borovsky, of Mag Noy Israel Ornamental Fish, demonstrates the proper way to handle a large koi to avoid injury.

CHLORINE AND CHLORAMINES

Municipally supplied water may contain chlorine and chloramines. It is wise to check with the municipal supplier to determine what chemicals are added to the water. The presence of chloramines in the water may provide a positive test result for ammonia. The presence of either chemical can severely stress and kill fish. Signs of chlorine toxicity in a fish are pale fins and a shakiness in its movement.

Providing aeration for two or three days will dissipate the chlorine from the water. Chloramines, however, can remain in the water for a long time. Chloramines are the product of chlorine combining with ammonia that has been added to the water supply. Hence, it is possible to record a toxic ammonia level straight from the tap. Commercial treatments are available for the removal of these chemicals. Follow the directions supplied with the product.

Adding zeolite to the filtration system will help to remove ammonia from chloramines. Total reliance on this method of removal, however, may take two weeks or longer, depending on pool size. Chloramine eliminators may not be adequately reliable in treating a significant volume of water, such as might be encountered in fifty percent water changes. After administering such treatment, wait ten or fifteen minutes and test the water for ammonia to determine the success of the treatment.

Topping off the pool with municipally supplied water can be hazardous to fish if performed frequently. Five percent water additions no more than once or twice weekly will probably not stress or harm fish. Such additions should be performed slowly as a light spray on the water's surface. The water should not be sprayed on aquatic plants. Check the ammonia level afterwards if chloramines are in the water. If such additions are made regularly, the concentration of ammonia may accumulate. Sufficient chlorine and chloramine eliminators to treat the pool should be kept on hand in the event of an emergency.

OXYGEN DEFICIENCY

If an oxygen test kit is not available, observing the fish's behavior is a good indication of the pond's oxygen supply. Gulping at the water's surface or gathering at the water outlet source are signs the oxygen level has lowered. The sudden unexplained death of fish overnight may indicate that oxygen depletion has become lethal. Additional aeration must be provided. A supplemental unit may be required, or it may simply be that the pump needs to be run twenty-four hours a day. Setting up a pump to discharge just below the water's surface will create additional aeration as will installing a diffuser bar on the pool's bottom. If air-stones are used, remember to soak them awhile before use.

Check the fish population. Too many fish may increase the oxygen requirements beyond the pool's capacity. Place excess fish in other homes, provide additional aeration, and monitor water quality.

If the water is particularly green, the problem may be that the algae are consuming too much oxygen at night. Provide additional aeration and treat for algae.

Check the surface coverage afforded by plants. If more than sixty percent of the surface is covered, there may be insufficient surface exposed to the air for adequate oxygen exchange. Provide additional aeration and/or remove some of the plants.

If fish display distress following heavy rains, the problem is likely to be the result of water "turnover." (See Chapter Six, "Oxygen Depletion," page 47.) Provide additional aeration. If the pool's water source is a well, the well water may be low in oxygen. Additions of such water should be made by spraying onto

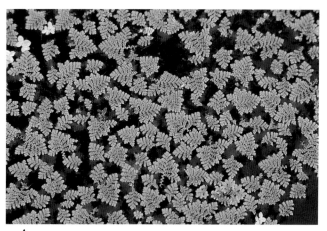

Azolla is not usually eaten by fish and can cover the pond's surface, resulting in oxygen depletion.

Vigorous water lilies can provide too much surface coverage and trap heat within the pond on hot summer days.

Fish gathering at the surface and gulping air are not being friendly—they need more oxygen.

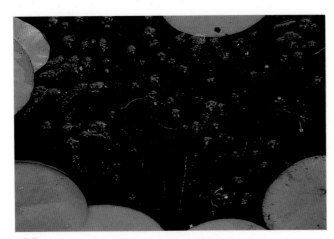

Uncontrolled Elodea sp. can deprive fish of both oxygen and space.

the pool's surface. Supplemental aeration may be necessary.

The start-up period of a bio-filter may produce temporary oxygen depletions. Provide additional aeration as needed.

If fish are indicating an oxygen depletion condition in the pool, do not feed them until the situation has been remedied. Food digestion increases the fish's oxygen requirements.

EXCESS CARBON DIOXIDE

Since too much carbon dioxide in the water prevents fish from accessing available oxygen, their behavior will be as though they were oxygen deprived. Excess carbon dioxide can be dissipated by aeration of the water.

CHANGES IN TEMPERATURE AND CLIMATE

Fish are usually weak in the early spring following their winter "hibernation." If the spring weather is erratic with fluctuating warm and cold spells, the changes in the water temperature will stress the fish even more, leaving them more vulnerable to disease and parasites. Once the water temperature rises above 50°F, a pool heater may be used to maintain that temperature and lessen the fish's stress.

Once the pool water has warmed to a consistent 50°F, the pool may be treated for parasites that naturally occur in the water and often attack winter-weakened fish. This treatment should be performed before activating the bio-filter as the medications will destroy the filter's bacteria. Once the treatment has

*W*ater clover (Marsilea *sp.) can become so invasive as to hamper or trap fish.*

been completed, any residual chemicals in the pool water should be neutralized, filtered out with activated charcoal, or removed from the water through partial water changes.

The bright, early days of spring may stress fish since plants have not yet grown enough to provide shelter. Aquatic blue dye can be used to shade the water and reduce their stress. An added benefit is that the dye may forestall the traditional algae bloom. Remember to move submerged aquatics closer to the pool's surface to access the sunlight they require for growth. The dye will later need to be diluted from the water by partial water changes.

AMMONIA AND NITRITE

Ammonia is a waste product given off by fish as well as a chemical added by many municipal water suppliers to produce disinfecting chloramines. Both ammonia and nitrite are products of the nitrogen cycle produced by decaying organic matter and excess fish foods. Even the slightest presence of ammonia or nitrite in the water will stress and weaken fish. An elevated presence of these two waste products will kill them.

Frequently, the cause of ammonia and nitrites being present in the water is an excess of fish. If the water tests for only a slight presence of ammonia and nitrite, and the fish population is in excess, it may be sufficient to relocate the excess fish and then monitor the water daily until the wastes are no longer reflected by testing. Providing additional filtration to accommodate the excess population may be impractical.

The second most frequent cause of positive testing for these waste products is poor pool hygiene. The pond should be kept free of dying vegetation that may quickly begin to decompose in the water. Excess fish food will settle to the pool bottom where it will also decompose. Some fish foods contain dust-size particles that only contaminate the pool. Feed fish only what they will consume in five minutes and avoid crumbly foods. Excess floating-type food is easily netted from the pool.

A heightened pH will amplify the toxicity of ammonia and nitrite by tenfold for each pH integer. A partial water change will dilute the toxicity. Additional remedies may have to be executed before determining the cause of the heightened pH.

A partial water change of as much as fifty percent of the pool's volume may be executed as an emergency measure. If the water source is municipally supplied, special precautions should be taken to counter the presence of chlorine and chloramines. It may be necessary to remove fish to a holding pond or hospital tank while treating the water.

Place zeolite in nylon stockings or mesh bags and drag them through the pool or suspend them at various points around the pond to remove ammonia until testing proves the ammonia has reached a safe level.

Nitrite levels may be lowered by the addition of two

to three tablespoons of non-iodized salt per five gallons of pool water. Dissolve the salt before adding it to the pool. During the initial start-up of a bio-filter, nitrite levels commonly rise. Add salt as suggested and continue to monitor the nitrite level until the bio-filter has begun converting it to nitrates.

If a pool is not monitored regularly, the effects of ammonia and nitrite may not be noticed until it is too late to save many of the fish. If a fish dies for no apparent reason, first test the water. If no presence of ammonia or nitrite is noted, then check for oxygen depletion and other possible causes.

The presence of a white goldfish or koi in the pool may act as a barometer of ammonia and nitrite presence. If these products are present, the fish will show stress, first showing a blushing and clamping of the fins. As the levels become more toxic and the fish's stress increases, the fish's body will show a red veining.

OVERPOPULATION

Fish do grow and multiply. What may have begun as an appropriate stocking level in the pool can increase to an overstocked level. Too many fish will create stress by depleting oxygen and excreting an excess of ammonia into the pool water. When the number and size of fish exceeds the recommended stocking level, excess fish should be removed from the pond and shared with friends, taken to a local pet store, kept in an aquarium, or placed in a new pool. Water gardening clubs and societies may offer a ready placement for fish. Domestic fish should never be released into the wild.

CHANGES IN WATER pH

A change in the water pH of more than 0.2 will stress fish. Do not artificially induce such changes. Some ponds will test with fluctuations of the pH from morning to afternoon. Usually this is an indication of green water algae. Goldfish and koi tolerate these fluctuations better than more sensitive fish such as orfe or rudd. The pool should be treated for the green water algae. If it appears that these fluctuations are stressing the fish, add a dissolved salt tonic of 2.5 g/l or 2 pounds per 100 gallons of pool water to relieve the stress.

Ponds with water testing slightly below the neutral pH of 7 may experience more fluctuations than more alkaline waters. These pools may be buffered to resist such fluctuations. However, buffering compounds of calcium carbonate or sodium bicarbonate essentially function as pH raisers. To determine the proper dosage, remove one gallon of pool water. Add the buffering compound one teaspoon at a time, testing the pH after each addition. Once the number of teaspoons to effect no more than a 0.2 rise in pH is known, convert that figure to the pond's volume. This dosage should be applied once a day until the desired reading is attained.

ACCLIMATING NEW FISH TO A CHANGE IN pH

New fish brought in from a different water supply may not be acclimated to the pH they will find in their new home. Especially if the fish are going to be placed directly into the pool, it is important to test the pH of both the fish's bagged water and the pool's water. If the two levels are more than 0.2 apart, it will be necessary to acclimate the fish in an aquarium or temporary quarters.

Fill the temporary tank with water from the pool. Use a commercial pH adjuster to make the tank's water within a 0.2 range of the bagged water. Float the bagged fish until the temperatures have equalized and release the fish into the tank. Be sure to provide aeration in the tank. If the fish is to remain in the tank for several days or for the two-week quarantine period, a filter may be set up with zeolite and floss or foam media.

Adjust the pH by no more than 0.2 a day towards the pool's pH. If the desired two-week quarantine period is being observed, the fish will be acclimated to the pool's pH by the end of that time.

NUTRITION

Pond fish have specific nutritional needs. Feeding an exclusive diet of an inappropriate food such as catfish pellets may weaken the fish and bring on signs of stress. As a general rule, during the warm summer months of energetic behavior, fish should be fed foods high in proteins. In preparation for the winter hibernation months when fish survive on stored body fat, wheat germ-type foods are recommended for their ease of digestibility with slowing metabolisms. Likewise, the resumption of feeding in the early spring

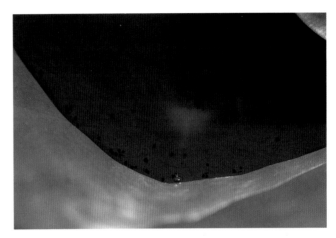

Tiny water insects, such as daphnia, are a natural food source of pond fish.

should not include high protein foods at the risk of inadequate digestion. While not as balanced as some commercial foods, Cheerios® is an acceptable food.

The digestion of food requires additional oxygen. Do not feed fish if the aeration pump is not working. When temperatures drop at night, the fish's metabolism slows. Feeding the fish late in the day and in the early evening can result in digestive problems.

Koi especially appreciate daily rations of fresh, tender salad greens. They will also feed upon filamentous algae, submerged aquatic plants, duckweed (*Lemna* sp.) and water lettuce (*Pistia* sp.), as well as the tender emerging growth of water lilies. While goldfish seldom create havoc by feeding on the pool's aquatics, they will freely eat duckweed, water lettuce, and elodea. Supplying fresh salad greens may help save these plants.

In a well-established pool, there will be sufficient food available, such as tubifex worms, blood worms, cyclops, and mosquito larvae for a balanced fish population. Providing additional foods may not be necessary and should be regulated to prevent its accumulation as waste in the pool. Live *Daphnia* and freshwater

Feeding fish floating pellets allows uneaten food to be netted from the pond before it can decompose.

Insect larvae are tasty treats for fish.

Hornwort (Ceratophyllum) *is a submerged floating plant that offers spawning areas for fish eggs.*

stress load and susceptibility to disease and parasites.

Executing water changes more than once weekly may prove stressful to fish, especially if the water changes exceed the recommended 5 percent. Any water change should be performed with care to avoid exposing the fish to drastic temperature changes. Abrupt temperature changes of but a few degrees create problems for fish.

shrimp can be cultivated in separate tanks for natural feedings.

REPEATED CHANGES IN ENVIRONMENTAL CONDITIONS

Any environmental change such as water quality, water temperature, and oxygen availability will stress fish. The repetition of such changes only increases the

USING SALT AS A FISH TREATMENT

All salt treatments should be effected with sea salt or non-iodized salt. Iodine concentrations can be toxic to fish.

Dosage	Objective
2.5 g/l or 2 lb/100 gal	Tonic for weak/ stressed fish
	Algae begin to die

3 g/l or 2.5 lb/100 gal or 1–2 T/5 gal	Detoxify nitrite
5 g/l or 4 lb/100 gal	Destroy pool parasites (2- to 3-week treatment)
8 oz/20 gal	Parasitic treatment with medications
10 g/l or 8 lb/100 gal	Treat fish ulcers Use with antibiotics 4-week treatment
20 g/l or 6 T/gal	Destroy parasites Use as 10-minute bath
1 lb/gal	Destroy parasites Use as 15-second dip
1 lb/3 gal	Disinfectant for injuries 10- to 15-second dip
1 tsp/5 gal	Antiseptic for open wounds

***D**ragonfly larvae are easily concealed in stone and pool detritus, where they prey upon other insects and fish fry.*

FISH EUTHANASIA

Dissolve two tablespoons of salt in a plastic bag of water. Place fish in the bag and store in the freezer for several hours or overnight. The salt serves to calm the fish as the water temperature lowers. With the lowering temperature, the fish's metabolism slows and its awareness decreases.

Several laboratories market chemicals that sedate fish. Normally used to slow the fish's metabolism to alleviate transport stress, these chemicals may be used

***S**everal species of dragonfly will visit the pond to lay their eggs in the pond water.*

at ten times the recommended dosage to humanely euthanize a fish.

THE HOSPITAL/ QUARANTINE TANK

Any new fish to be added to the pool should be closely observed first for two full weeks. Always assume a new fish is infected with parasites. Be especially cautious of adding "feeder" goldfish to the pool. Since these fish are bred to be part of the food chain, less care may have been taken to ensure their good health. If the new fish are the only fish in the pool, the entire pool may be treated. Otherwise, it is less expensive, as well as more manageable, to treat a new fish in a smaller, more observable body such as a glass aquarium.

A glass aquarium may be set up as a hospital tank. It should be equipped with at least an aeration device, usually an air pump with an airstone attached. A recirculating filter may also be used, but should be equipped with only ammonia-adsorbing media and filter floss or foam. Activated charcoal will immediately filter any medications from the water. Since many medications require vigorous aeration, the air pump may still be required with the presence of an aquarium filter. To determine the fish-holding capacity of the aquarium, compute the square surface area of the tank in inches. Divide this figure by 30 to determine the number of body inches the tank can accommodate. Since overcrowding is also stressful, it is important not to add this factor to an already stressed and sick fish.

New fish should be treated with a broad-spectrum parasite medication. Antibiotics should not be used unless a specific disease is noticed. One or two tablespoons of salt per five gallons of water will assist in relieving stress as well as in treating for parasites. If medications are not available, the 5 g/l dosage of salt

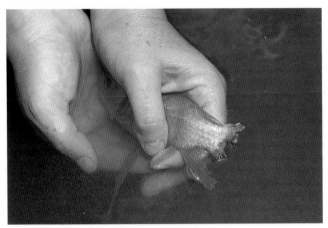

A white, tufty fungal growth attacks this weakened fish.

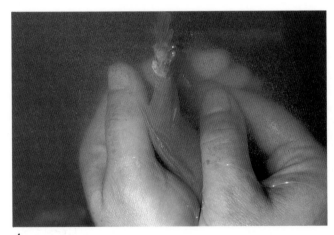

Anchor worms and tail rot are encouraged by poor water conditions.

for the two-week period may suffice.

The water temperature in a hospital tank should be maintained at a stable level close to that of the pool. However, if only a salt treatment is used to destroy possible parasites, it may be desirable to use an aquarium heater for the two-week period to heat the tank to 86 to 93°F. The temperature should not be raised more than one degree per hour to avoid risking the fish.

Such temperatures will kill most parasites. Following the treatment period, the tank water should be allowed to cool to the pool's temperature before transferring the fish. (See "Home Remedies," page 119.)

Maintain good aeration during treatments. If the fish is affected by parasites, it may be weakened and have a greater oxygen need. If new fish cannot be quarantined, the entire pool should be treated with a broad-spectrum parasiticide for a two- to three-week period. Closely observe the fish during this period.

New fish should be observed for signs of skin lesions, raised scales, protruding eyes, open wounds, rapid breathing, white spots, frayed fins, skin or eye cloudiness, and scratching behavior. If the fish continue to feed with the presence of symptoms, the problem is likely to be parasites. If the fish are not feeding, the problem is likely to be protozoan.

Never leave a fish in medicated water longer than is recommended. Never leave a fish unattended if it is immersed in short-term baths or dips. Remove the fish

Decking that extends over the pond can provide welcome shade to fish during the early warming days of spring.

immediately if it displays signs of great stress or attempts to jump from the bath.

Always disinfect nets between uses. One or two drops of formaldehyde per gallon of water may be kept in a closed container throughout the season for this purpose. (Label the container and keep it out of the reach of children.)

The hospital tank should be thoroughly cleaned and disinfected after its use.

TEMPORARY FISH QUARTERS

In treating a large fish or a number of fish, the use of an aquarium may not be practical. Temporary quarters for fish may be built of wooden planks supported by concrete blocks to accommodate a water depth of 9 to 12 inches. A depth of 12 inches will facilitate volume computations for medication dosages. A double sheet of polyethylene is draped and secured in the frame. Shade should be provided in warm, sunny weather. A net or a screen over the top will prevent fish from jumping out and predators from getting in. A small pool pump or aquarium air pump helps to maintain oxygen supply.

DETECTING FISH DISEASES AND PROBLEMS

Signs of disease or infections:
• Loss of appetite
• Fins clamped close to body
• Swimming weakly close to the water's surface or off by itself
• Nipping or bumping of affected fish by other fish when not spawning
• Increased gill movements
• Visual changes in fins, skin, or eyes
• Increased mucous production on body
• Blushing of fins or red streaking on body
• Scratching on pool walls, rocks, etc. (flashing)
• Jumping from the water or out of the pool when not spawning

First check the basics of the fish's environment:
• Ammonia and nitrite levels
• Sufficient aeration and oxygen
• Presence of chlorine and/or chloramines
• Presence of predators
• Electrical shocking
• Presence of toxic run-off entering water
• Presence of lime or marble chips

In addition to displaying one of the signs of disease or infection, the fish may develop sores at the site of a parasitic attack. Swab the wound with Mercurochrome or another safe antiseptic. Secondary bacterial infections or fuzzy tufts of fungal infections may aggravate the initial condition and necessitate additional treatments for these conditions.

The life cycle of parasites is temperature-dependent. Because the life cycle of most parasites involves a period of encystation during which treatment is not effective, the treatments must encompass the full life cycle. Consequently, temperatures below 50°F involve too long a period of time in the parasitic life cycle to effect treatment. Be wary of commercial medications that imply only one treatment is necessary. Depending on the water temperature, additional treatments will be required over a two- to four-week period to prevent re-infection.

Poor pool hygiene may invite continued infestations as the parasites' eggs will accumulate in organic debris on the pool bottom or in the filter media. Such debris should be removed regularly by vacuuming the pool bottom and cleaning the filter unit as needed.

DIPS AND BATHS

Many treatments for disease or infestations offer a dosage for dips or baths in lieu of full-pond treatments. To effect a dip treatment, the fish is left within the net and suspended in the solution for the specified treatment time. Upon removal from the solution, the fish should be rinsed by dipping in clean water or gently spraying away the medication residue to prevent the burning of tissue.

In a bath treatment, the fish is released into the

Deep-bodied fish, such as this redcap oranda, have limited movement and can be easy prey in the backyard pond.

solution for a period of time. Aeration usually must be supplied. Because baths are normally of weak solutions, the treatment may not be fully effective. Repeated treatments in such weak solutions may assist the pathogen's development of resistance to the treatment. Hence, in the case of repeated treatments, alternating medications may be wise.

GENERAL GUIDELINES FOR MEDICATING FISH

If a hospital tank is being used, it should be filled with water from the pool, unless the water quality is not good. The temperature of the water should be the same as that from which the fish is being removed.

The tank should be protected from direct sunlight. Medications should not be performed on hot days when the water's oxygen content is lower, since treatments increase the fish's need for oxygen. Supplemental aeration is usually required for effective treatment. If an airstone is used for this purpose, it must be soaked awhile before connecting the pump.

Many dosages are presented in terms of milliliters. The local pharmacist may be able to supply a dropper so calibrated. A standard eye dropper will deliver approximately 20 drops of water per milliliter. Stock solutions may be produced by dissolving one gram of medication in one liter of water, making each milliliter of the solution contain one milligram of the drug.

Remember that chemicals and medications are effective because they are toxic. The toxicity to parasites is simply of a lower tolerance than the fish's. Follow dosage instructions exactly. Avoid regular preventive treatments or underdosing to prevent the parasites' acquiring resistance to the medications. In using a new treatment or unfamiliar drug, it may be wise to test the fish's tolerance by first testing it on a weaker affected fish.

UV sterilizers can break down medications and should be turned off during treatment. Since activated carbon will remove many medications from water, such filtration should not be used with the treatment. Bio-filters should be disconnected from the treated water, as well, to prevent the medication from destroying the nitrifying bacteria.

At the conclusion of a whole-pool treatment, frequent small water changes of ten to twenty percent for several days, along with filtration by activated charcoal, will remove any residual drugs from the water. Snails and, in some instances, tadpoles may be adversely affected by medications administered in the pond. If they have been removed, they should not be returned until the water is fairly clear of the medication.

COMMON PARASITIC INFESTATIONS

The following descriptions are of common parasitic crustaceans and flukes that may attack pool fish. While it may be helpful to determine what specifically is attacking the fish, the treatments for parasites are basically the same. Remember that with parasitic infestations, fish may show a variety of symptoms, but will continue to remain active and to feed.

- Fish lice (*Argulus*) appear as clear, gelatinous, round-shaped objects up to 0.4 inches in length with visible legs and eye spots. They may be easily removed by patting the fish gently with a cotton swab soaked in full-strength tincture of iodine. (Kerosene and turpentine should not be used.) This may be a desired procedure to prevent the fish from injuring itself while the pool is being treated for the parasites.
- Anchor worms (*Lernea*) are stick-like parasites up to 0.8 inches long with two egg sacs at the posterior end and a hook-like head that attaches to the fish. Chemical treatments will kill only the free-swimming stage of the parasite and will not affect the worm itself or its eggs. The worm should be carefully removed with tweezers, the wound swabbed with Mercurochrome, and the fish dipped for ten to fifteen seconds in a salt bath of one pound of salt to three gallons of water.
- Skin flukes (*Gyrodactylus* sp.) are not easily seen as they are only .02 to .04 inches. They cause a greyish

mucus to be produced on the fish's body. If the flukes are on the fins, the fins will twitch. If the flukes are inside the mouth, the fish will open and close its mouth quickly as if trying to remove them. Generally, the fish will make quick, startled movements followed by scratching.

- Gill flukes (*Dactylogyrus* sp.) appear on the gill filaments as tiny dark spots from .04 to .08 inches long. Severe infestations cause the gills to become inflamed and to appear white and puffy.
- Gill maggots (*Ergasilus* sp.) appear as greyish black and white parasites several millimetres long massed about the gills.

CHEMICAL TREATMENTS FOR PARASITIC INFESTATIONS

Commercial products containing one or more of the following: malachite green, acriflavine, dimetridazole, methylene blue, formalin, metronidazole, quinine, or organophosphate chemicals. Organophosphate chemicals are lethal to orfe and rudd.

The above products will kill all free-swimming infective stages of parasites as well as adult parasites with the exception of anchor worms and parasitic eggs. Do not exceed recommended dosages. Overdoses can cause nerve damage or death to fish. Whenever possible, conduct treatments within a hospital tank to monitor adverse or stress reactions.

A complete treatment involves **five** applications of the correct dosage at the recommended intervals to accommodate the temperature-dependent life cycle of the parasites.

- Above 80°F, once every 3 to 4 days.
- Between 70°F and 80°F, once every 7 days.

• Between 50°F and 60°F, once every 10 to 14 days.

• Below 50°F, the parasite's life cycle is too long for effective treatment. Treatment should be delayed until the temperature has warmed sufficiently.

If the entire pool is being treated, the bio-filter should be disconnected to prevent the treatment chemicals from destroying the nitrifying bacteria. Non-iodized salt may be used in conjunction with the chemical treatments at a ratio of 8 ounces of salt per 20 gallons of water. A fifty percent water change should be effected weekly during the course of treatment. If chemicals are not used, a salt treatment alone may prove effective with light parasitic infestations.

Formaldehyde or formalin should not be used on fish with open sores as the chemical is lethal if it enters the fish's body. Potassium permanganate can be used for crustacean and fluke infestations as a bath with a ratio of 5 to 10 ppm for one hour. As a total pool treatment, 3 to 5 ppm may be used. The coloration of the water disappears in time, so that water changes are not necessary.

Americans, unaccustomed to the metric system, can be frustrated by the term "parts per million" (ppm) since it means the number of milligrams per liter. To determine how much potassium permanganate to use for the 5 ppm dosage suggested above, we begin by needing 5 milligrams per liter. We will use a 10-gallon aquarium for the treatment. A 10-gallon aquarium holds the equivalent of 37.85 liters. Since we need 5 milligrams per liter, we must multiply 37.85 by five, which gives 189.25 milligrams. Lacking a measuring spoon that measures milligrams, we must convert the milligrams into grains; one grain equals 64.8 milligrams. Dividing 189.25 milligrams by 64.8 grains per milligram tells us that approximately 3 grains are required. The dosage range suggested above is 5 to 10 ppm, which means 3 to 6 grains of potassium permanganate would be required in a 10-gallon aquarium.

Since cookbooks list "a few" grains as equal to less than ⅛ teaspoon, a small pinch will effect the needed dosage. (When using the Appendix for equivalents, do not confuse liquid and dry measures.)

If the fish has not responded to treatment within three to five days, the problem may have been misdiagnosed. See treatment for protozoan infestations.

COMMON PROTOZOAN INFESTATIONS

Protozoan infestations are not visible to the naked eye. The most commonly encountered are ich, chilodonella, oodinium ocellatum, epistylus, and trichondina. Early signs are a general lethargy, loss of appetite, and scratching or flashing. The fish may appear to gasp for air or place itself near the pool's waterfall. Close observation of the fish's eyes or fins may show a cloudiness or tiny white spots. As the infestation worsens, the fish may produce extra mucous coating in an effort to protect itself. A severe infestation will be indicated by red veins appearing on the fish's skin. Protozoan life cycles are temperature-dependent, lasting only two days in 80°F water and up to two months in the winter.

The most common protozoan infestation is ich, which appears as white powdery spots on the fish's body and gills. The winter stage of the infestation appears as a globular waxy patch. Only the free-swimming stage is treatable. Oodinium appears similar to ich, but exhibits yellowish spotting.

Epistylus can cause localized damage that results in bacterial hole-in-the-side disease. This infestation is characterized by a thick, localized mucus production around a white area rimmed with red on the fish's body.

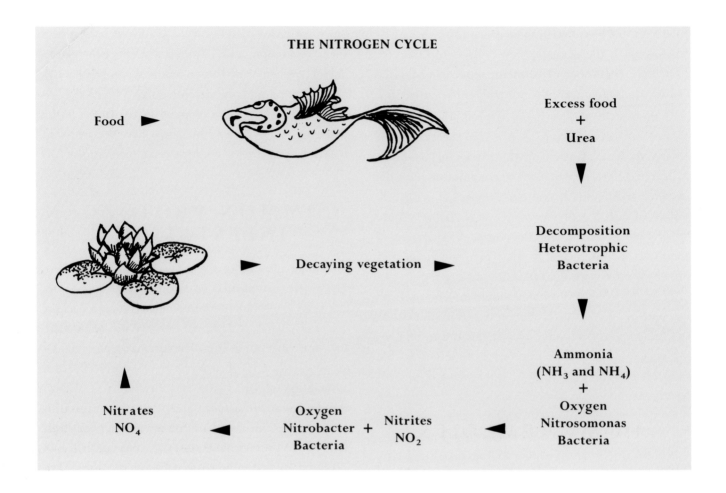

THE NITROGEN CYCLE

Food ▶

Excess food
+
Urea

▼

Decomposition
Heterotrophic
Bacteria

▼

Decaying vegetation ▶

Ammonia
(NH_3 and NH_4)
+
Oxygen
Nitrosomonas
Bacteria

Nitrates
NO_4

◀

Oxygen
Nitrobacter +
Bacteria

Nitrites
NO_2

◀

CHEMICAL TREATMENTS FOR PROTOZOAN INFESTATIONS

A complete treatment program for protozoan infestations requires four applications of the appropriate dosage of formalin or malachite green. (Safer medications are under development.) Since only the free-swimming stages are treatable, the program must be continued over a long enough period to destroy the progression of the encysted and egg forms of the infestation. Heavy infestations may not be relieved until after the second or third treatment. Since weak and heavily infested fish may not survive, early treatment is important. Trichodina may have an acquired immunity to the standard treatments and may require an alternative remedy.

Using the dosages recommended with the product, the following treatment schedule should be followed:

• At temperatures near 64°F, treat 5 days apart for 20 days total.

• At temperatures around 72°F, treat once every 3 days for 12 days total.

• At temperatures below 50°F, the parasite's life cycle is too long for effective treatment.

A 200 ppm solution of formaldehyde or formalin may be used as a bath treatment. (To figure the dosage to administer in a 10-gallon aquarium, multiply 37.85 liters by 200, which gives 7,570 milligrams, the number required for 200 ppm. Divide 7,570 by 1,000, to determine that 7.57 grams are needed. Since one gram equals .0353 dry ounce measure, multiply this figure by 7.57, to determine that 0.27 ounces or approximately ¼ oz. of the medication is required to effect the proper dosage.)

Aerate the solution vigorously for 10 to 15 minutes before immersing the fish. Aeration continues during the one-hour treatment. If the fish shows signs of distress, remove it at once. This treatment may be performed more than once daily, if necessary. Do not exceed the recommended dosage.

An alternative treatment of chelated copper may be used to treat protozoan cryptocaron and oodinium infestations. One teaspoon or 5 ml per 10 gallons of water will produce a 0.25 ppm concentration.

HOME REMEDIES

Most parasites will be killed by a water temperature of 86 to 93°F. The affected fish should be placed in a hospital tank of pool water. Using an aquarium heater, slowly heat the water to the desired level by increasing the temperature no more than one degree per hour. An in-tank or tape thermometer on the tank's outside glass provides the necessary monitoring. The fish should be kept at the elevated temperature at least 24 hours for oodinium, four days for costia, and ten days for ich. The water temperature may then be lowered gradually back to that of the pool. As an extra precaution, the fish may be dipped in a salt solution for 10 to 15 seconds before returning to the pool. Watch the fish for the next two to three weeks for signs of recurrence.

A three percent solution of hydrogen peroxide may be used to treat skin parasites and protozoan infestations. 17.5 gm/l may be used in a 10–15 minute bath.

5000 ppm may be used as a 5-minute dip. Tincture of iodine in a ten percent solution may be used as a disinfectant for skin wounds and injuries.

A 0.05% to 0.1% salt solution may be used to control ich infestations without disrupting the biofilter. A 10% solution of vinegar affords protection from external protozoa, fish lice, and leeches. 1500 mg/l may be used as a 5–10 minute dip. 2000 mg/l may be used for a 45–60 second dip. 500 mg/l may be used as a 30-minute bath.

Lilac leaves placed in mesh bags are an antiprotozoal agent. Pine needles enclosed within nylon stockings may provide protection from ich protozoa.

TREATING FUNGAL INFECTIONS

Fungal infections appearing as tufts of cotton are usually caused by *Saprolegnia* sp. These infections often occur as a secondary phase following injury or stress. Low water temperatures seem to make a fish more susceptible to fungal attacks. Malachite green or copper sulfate is used for fungal treatments.

Malachite green can be harmful to fish and humans if it is used improperly. The fish may be treated in a hospital tank in a solution of 7 milligrams of malachite green to one gallon of water for two hours. The pool itself may be treated with a ratio of 1 milligram of malachite green to 3 liters of water. No water change or removal of the fish is required.

Copper sulfate may be used as a one- to two-minute bath as a solution of 0.5 milligrams of copper sulfate to one liter of water. Potassium permanganate, at a ratio of 1 gram to 10 gallons of water, may also be effective. The water need not be changed as the potassium permanganate dissipates in a short period of time. N-dodecylguandine acetate at a ratio of 4 mg/l is also effective.

DROPSY OR PINECONE DISEASE

Dropsy is a condition in which the fish appears to puff up with its scales standing out from the body. It is thought to be caused by bacteria, but does not appear to be a contagious condition. Kanacyn and tetracycline (Aquatronics), as well as Furan-2 (Aquarium Pharmaceuticals), are reported as effective treatments. In the later stages of the disease, the fish appears grotesque and lethargic. If the medication seems ineffective, euthanasia may be the most humane treatment.

BACTERIAL INFECTIONS

Common bacterial infections are indicated by fin and tail rot, excessive body slime, eye clouding, mouth fungus, and body sores. Treatments for minor bacterial infections include commercial broad-spectrum treatments containing one or more of the following: malachite green, acriflavine/ethacridine, methylene blue, formaldehyde or formalin, and sodium chloride. Topical treatments may also be effective.

Antibacterial and antibiotic treatments for severe infections should be administered in both the fish's food and water. Food treatments include oxolinic acid, oxytetracycline, and other quinoline antibacterials. Water treatments include nifurpirinol, sodium nifurstyrenate, oxytetracycline, and ampicillin.

A recipe for medicated fish food:

Ingredients

1 cup goldfish or koi food pellets
⅔ cup water
1 packet unflavored gelatin
1½ grams medicated powder

Directions

1. Use a blender to convert fish pellets into powder.
2. Boil water and add gelatin. Stir until dissolved.
3. Cool gelatin until lukewarm.
4. Add medicated powder and stir well.
5. Add powdered pellets and stir well.
6. Flatten into ½-inch-square cakes and store in an airtight bag in the refrigerator.
7. Feed one cake per 12-inch fish for 10 days. Feed to sick fish only, if possible.

Because antibiotics generally have very short shelf lives, they should be used immediately after mixing. They should always be administered within a glass hospital tank. Since it is important to observe treated fish for signs of toxicity and oxygen depletion, antibiotics should not be administered at night. They should not be flushed into municipal water supplies. They can be decomposed by baking in a warm oven (130 degrees) for two days.

TOPICAL ANTIBACTERIAL TREATMENTS

Fish can be injured, particularly during spawning. Cold-blooded pond fish should be treated in water over 55°F since they cannot heal at lower temperatures.

The following topical antibacterial treatments may be used in treating open wounds and sores: tincture of iodine, povidone-iodine, Mercurochrome, proprietary treatments containing bensalkonium chloride, and proprietary antibacterial, antibiotic, and protective pastes and ointments.

As with any other medicinal treatment, large amounts may be toxic. Care should be taken to prevent the medications from getting into the fish's gills. Always rinse medicated fish before returning them to the pool.

POTASSIUM PERMANGANATE TREATMENTS

Potassium permanganate may be used in the treatment of external parasites, all common protozoan infestations, skin lesions and bacterial infections, and fungi.

As a disinfectant, potassium permanganate is mixed with water at a ratio of 1 gram to 50 liters. It may be used in the pool itself at a ratio of three to five milligrams per liter indefinitely. Always provide good aeration when using. When the color fades, the product has dissipated.

One gram per 10 liters may be used as a 5- to 10-second dip.

One gram per liter may be used as a 30–45 second dip.

One gram per 100 liters may be used as a 90-minute bath.

Particularly alkaline water will result in manganese precipitating onto the fish's gills. A high organic content in the water may alter the effectiveness of the treatment.

FORMALIN OR FORMALDEHYDE TREATMENTS

37–40% solutions of formaldehyde may be used to treat external protozoans, flukes, leeches, and fungi. Formaldehyde should be used with rubber gloves as it is a known carcinogen. Likewise, fumes from the chemical can irritate the respiratory passages. Formaldehyde will evaporate from water. A 15–20 mg/l ratio

may be kept indefinitely in the pool.

Other useful ratios using 37–40% formaldehyde:

1 ppm = 0.0038 ml/gal

15 ppm = 0.057 ml/gal

20 ppm = 0.076 ml/gal

25 ppm = 0.095 ml/gal

DISPOSAL OF CHEMICALLY TREATED WATERS

Excess medications and chemically treated waters should be carefully discarded where they will not enter the groundwater supply or the municipal water supply. They should not be disposed of through a municipally supplied sewage system. A site safe from family pets and other animals should be selected that will allow the chemicals to be naturally filtered from the water before it enters a water supply system.

A stock solution of 22.8 grams of potassium permanganate to 4 ounces of water at a rate of 2 drops per gallon to yield 5 ppm can be used to neutralize some medications such as malachite green.

Ironically, the real threat to municipal water supplies lies not in the disposal of chemically treated pool and aquarium waters, but in the discharge of salt-treated waters. Calcium chloride and magnesium chloride formed by salt additions weaken the chlorine added to municipal supplies. Suppliers must then add heavier chlorine concentrations or resort to adding ammonia to create chloramines.

Tropical fish, such as the red swordtail, gourami, and common guppy, enjoy a summer visit in the pond if the bottom temperature is at least 70°F.

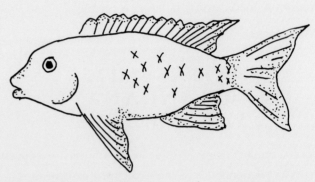

The *Sarotherodon mossambicus* is an excellent pond fish in climates too warm for goldfish.

FISH-CARE CALENDAR FOR TEMPERATE CLIMATES

January–February

Fish are surviving on stored food reserves in their bodies. Allow them to rest undisturbed. Do not feed them, even on occasional warm days when they may swim about. Feeding should not be resumed until the water temperature has stabilized above 50°F, since the lower winter metabolism cannot handle food digestion. Keep an opening in the ice to allow gas exchanges. Do not break ice as concussions may injure fish. Fish death at this time will be due to overpopulation, improper cleaning of the pool, or a buildup of methane and hydrogen sulfide gases beneath the ice.

March

Provide additional aeration of the water if the fish swim to the surface. Note that hungry fish gather near the surface in the area in which they are accustomed to being fed. They will actively search for food. Opening their mouths at the surface indicates a need for oxygen. If you offer food, keep it light and easily digestible. Avoid high protein foods. If the pool has been covered, remove the cover on a sunny day. If the pool is drained for cleaning, provide safe, quiet, temporary quarters for fish. Provide them with shelter from strong sunlight and treat the water with a Stress Coat and/or salt to alleviate stress.

April–May

Temperature changes in the water may leave the fish susceptible to parasites. Observe fish for signs of parasites or treat the entire pool. Temperature changes will stimulate spawning. Chasing and bumping each other is common. If fry are desired, it may be wise to net them out and tend them in an aquarium until they have reached sufficient size to prevent their consumption by larger fish and frogs. Stock the pool with daphnia or freshwater shrimp to provide nutrients for fish and fry. Begin feeding protein foods. Begin weekly five percent water changes while vacuuming wastes from the pool bottom.

The mosquito fish *(Gambusia)*, a small fish useful in warm climate areas, is an aggressive fin-nipper.

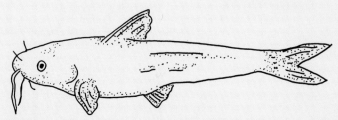

The albino catfish requires a larger pond to accommodate its mature size of 2–3 feet. Catfish will attack the eyes and fins of goldfish.

June

Periods of heat or rain can affect water quality. Be prepared to provide additional aeration if fish surface to request more oxygen. If feeding fish, feed only what they will consume in a five-minute period. Food should be high in protein. Supplement the fish's diet with fresh, tender salad greens or celery leaves. Spawning can continue every 2 to 3 weeks.

July–August

Since warmer water contains lesser amounts of oxygen, continue to monitor fish behavior. Especially on hot days, spraying the pool's surface with a hose may help cool and aerate the water. Excessive plant cover may cause the water to overheat. Fish may be fed as hunger indicates. Spawning may continue every 2 to 3 weeks.

September–October

Move any cold-water-sensitive fish to indoor aquariums. Decrease feeding as the temperature falls and the fish's activity slows. Feeding should be tapered to a light feeding once every 2 to 3 days by the end of October. Replace high protein foods with wheat germ types. If the water temperature drops to 50°F, stop feeding altogether. Keep pool free of fallen leaves and dying vegetation. Vacuum the pool bottom of any decaying vegetation. Monitor fish for signs of parasites as water temperature changes. Since parasitic life cycles will be slowed to a point of ineffective treatment, either wait until warming waters occur in the spring, or net out affected fish and treat in a hospital tank. To return fish to the pool, fill a plastic bag with water from the pool and allow it to warm to the temperature of the water in the fish's aquarium. Transfer the fish to the bag and float it in the pool until the temperature is equalized. Move any excess fish to other quarters.

November–December

Feed lightly only once weekly until water temperature reaches 50°F and then stop feeding. If the pump is kept running through the winter, raise it to within a foot of the pool's surface to prevent overcooling of the lower water. Be certain all possible decaying vegetation has been removed. Provide for keeping an open hole in the ice. Set up a plastic tent over pool, if desired.

chapter ten

INSECTS AND CRUSTACEANS

*The dragonfly (Odonata) rarely pauses in its
search for insects around the pond.*

After several moltings, the dragonfly nymph climbs from the water and leaves its final casing behind.

Even though water gardening resources list particular aquatic insects as pests, those commonly listed are but single members of oftentimes large families of insects. Many members of any insect family will display a particular characteristic or behavior. The China mark moth, for example, is an oft-cited pest that is predominantly of European occurrence. Yet pond-owners in other parts of the world will also observe the chewed leaves and floating shelters characteristic of the mark moth. Assuming that the average pond-owner is not a serious student of entomology, the primary concern is to identify insect families that may present problems in the backyard pool.

Aquatic insects that visit the pond will, for the most part, be flies, moths, and beetles. In many cases, the adult insect does not create a problem; it is the larval form that causes damage in the pool.

For the purpose of determining their impact on the pond, insect pests are considered predators, detritivores, and herbivores. Predators feed on other living organisms, including fish. Detritivores feed on pool detritus or decomposing organic matter on the pool bottom. Herbivores feed on living plant material.

If the pool bottom is regularly cleaned, detritivores such as some caddis flies, mayflies, stoneflies, and many midges will not be present for any length of time. And even if they are present, they will not pose a threat to fish or plants.

PREDATORS

Most predaceous insect larvae prey on other insects (including their own species), microorganisms, and tiny crustaceans. The larvae of mosquitoes, black flies, deer flies, horseflies, some caddis flies and mayflies, stoneflies, dobsonflies, alderflies, fishflies, darners, damselflies, dragonflies, whirligig beetles, water scavenger beetles, and several midges, including the bloodworm chironomid larvae, are all such predators. In addition, water bugs such as the water boatman and the water strider or water skater will prey on other insects. The larger of these larvae, such as the dragonfly (*Odonata*), will attack small fish. The adult forms of the water strider (*Gerridae*) and the water boatman (*Corixidae*) are known to attack small fish. However, for the most part, these predaceous insects will not present much of a problem in the pool.

Leeches appear initially to be worms, but closer observation reveals them to be flat with an ability to stretch and elongate. Very young leeches may appear as little more than a pinpoint on the underside of a lily leaf. Disturbing the leaf will encourage the tiny leeches to stretch and attempt to flee, making them more visible. True blood-sucking fish leeches are rarely seen in the backyard pool. What leeches that may enter the pool through plants are a common red-to-brown variety that scavenges and feeds upon other insects. Since it is good practice to disinfect new plants before adding them to the pool, a thorough hosing and wipedown, as well as a precautionary treatment with a

***A**dult whirligig beetles multiply rapidly in the pond, partially because of the distasteful substance they emit that makes them undesirable as food.*

broad-spectrum parasiticide, will help prevent the introduction of leeches into the pool. Leeches already present in the pool may be trapped by enclosing a piece of raw meat or chicken liver in a perforated plastic tub. Attach a string to the tub and suspend it overnight in the pool. Adding 3 to 4 ounces of dissolved, non-iodized salt per gallon of water will usually kill the leeches.

Certain families of insects extend their predaceous

behavior to include tadpoles, snails, smaller fish, and frogs:

- Backswimmers (*Notonectidae*), characterized by submerged upside-down swimming, water scorpions (*Nepidae*), and the giant water bugs (*Belostomatidae*), characterized by hanging from the water's surface by the tips of their abdomen, are true bugs that are predaceous in both their nymph and adult stages.
- The Great Diving Beetle and the Silver Diving Beetle are but two species of the *Dytiscidae* family. This family of beetles is characterized by their diving habit and by their surfacing to take in air by their mouth. Like the Giant Water Bug, diving beetles can inflict painful bites. The larvae of this beetle family, known as "water tigers," will also attack fish. The insect forms of these predators should be netted from the pool. Vegetable oil or cottonseed oil may be cast as a film upon the water's surface to cause the surface breathers to suffocate. An underwater pool lamp or a light near the pool will attract both the Giant Water Bug and the diving beetle, among others, for capture.
- The presence of water scorpions and their bottom-preying larvae is curtailed by keeping the pond bottom free of detritus that provides them safe harbor.

HERBIVORES

Herbivorous insects usually cause the greatest problems in the pool with their disfigurement and destruction of aquatic plants. Any chemical treatment of these insects should be performed outside the pool as any insecticides, including pyrethrum, are deadly to fish.

The presence of the aquatic leaf beetle (*Donacia*) is usually first noticed by tiny red rings encircling holes on the lily leaf. These holes are made by the adult beetle in order to access the underside of the leaf for depositing its eggs. The eggs hatch in 1–2 weeks into grublike larvae that feed upon thin-walled plant tissue. During later stages, the larvae feed upon stems and lily roots. A mid-summer repotting may disclose pupae among the plant's roots. Besides chewing holes in the lily leaves, the beetle larvae also disfigure the leaves with a stipple effect produced by the insertion of sharp terminal spurs to acquire oxygen from the leaf's tissue. A few species of the beetle, such as the *Galerucell nymphaea*, will lay eggs on top of the lily leaves.

The best way to prevent damage by aquatic leaf beetles is to regularly wipe the eggs from the leaves and stems. Eggs laid on top of the leaves can be removed by hosing. Knocking the eggs free of the leaves removes the larvae from their food source and makes them more available to fish and predaceous insects. The underside eggs can also be removed by rubbing them free with the thumb. They are easily transferred to a plastic margarine tub for destruction outside the pool.

Bacillus thuringiensis (B.t.) may be sprayed on the lily leaves if holes are noticed. If the larvae contact the bacteria, they become parasitized and will die. Avoid spraying the B.t. in the pond water.

The many holes in the leaves of this "Indiana" water lily betray the invasion of aquatic leaf beetles.

FEEDING HABITS OF AQUATIC INSECTS

1. **boring—herbivores (caterpillars, midges)**
2. **filtering—detritivores (mayflies)**
3–4. **capturing—predators (dragonflies, beetles)**
5. **trapping—detritivores, predators (caddis flies)**
6. **floating—herbivores (moths)**

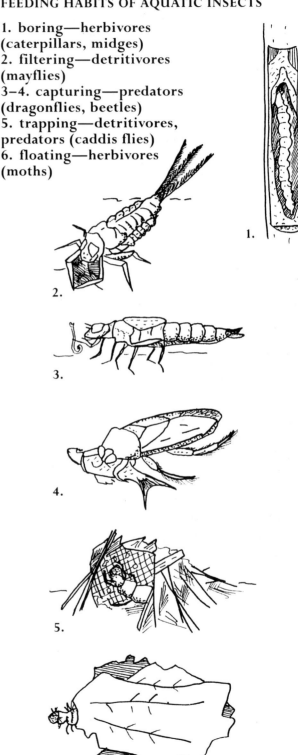

Chemicals such as malathion may be used if they are applied completely away from the pool. Keeping the plant(s) in a tub of systemic insecticide treatment for several days may reduce borer attacks. Never spray insecticides into the pond.

If holes are noticed in the lily leaves, it is still advisable to remove and dispose of them. Even if a very tiny larva were not at work, the action would be prudent for removing invitations to moths to lay their eggs in so accessible a place.

Leaf mining midges (*Chironomus*) visit the pool in the evening as swarms of what appear to be mosquito-like insects. They deposit their eggs in the water, where the hatched larvae find their way to lily leaves. Tunnelling through the leaves as they feed, the larvae leave behind rotted-edged cuttings in the leaves. Pygmy varieties of lilies may perish from such infestations. Any affected leaves should be removed and destroyed immediately. Installing a bat house or a purple marten house will invite resident sentries who will help keep the insects under control. An electric bug-light near the pool will also help.

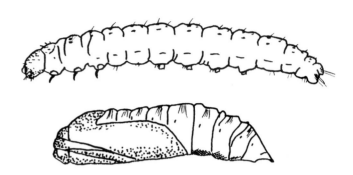

Ostrina *(pyraustinae)* larvae and pupae, the lotus borer, will ravage both lotus and water lilies.

The false leaf-mining midge (*Cricoptopus*) differs in that it does not tunnel completely through the leaf. This larva feeds only on the surface of the leaf and leaves a meandering tracery that will eventually rot through. These minute larvae may be knocked from the leaf with a strong hosing.

Both types of midges may be treated with nicotine or malathion baths to the affected plants away from the pool. Rinse the plants with clean water before return-

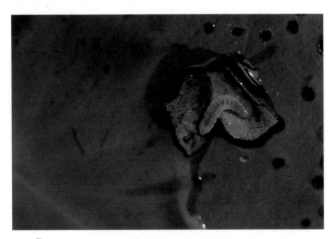

Several species of moths build shelters of leaf pieces and debris, from which they feed on the water's surface.

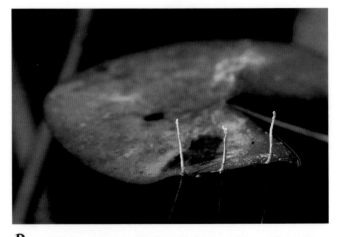

Rattailed maggots (Eristalis) are always found on foliage at the water's surface, where they have access to air.

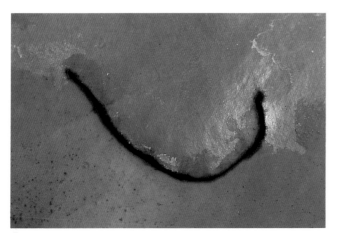

Leaf miners tunnel through or on the surface of lily leaves and leave behind rotting and disfiguring trails.

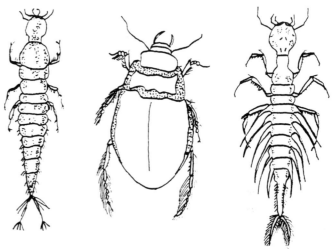

Diving beetles and their larvae will prey upon fish in the pond.

Aquatic leaf beetle (Chrysomelidae, Donacia) eggs are laid neatly on the undersides of lily leaves. The emerging larvae will pierce the leaf with double air-breathing tubes.

by trimming and destroying the affected plant part. Standard insecticides may be applied away from the pool area.

ing them to the pool. Do not use radically colder water for the treatment or the rinsing.

Various members of the moth family visit the pool in the evening hours to feed upon plant liquids. Eggs will be laid on the undersides of the water lily leaves, often radially around holes previously made by the leaf beetle. The eggs hatch into tiny mining caterpillars that burrow into the lily leaves and leave rotting traceries. The caterpillars often find their way into the leaf petiole or stem. Some will burrow their way down into the plant root. Others chew off bits of the leaf to form a flat larva case from which they feed upon the edges of leaves as they float about the pool. All aquatic plants in the pond are susceptible to attack by various moth larvae. (See remedies listed above.)

Certain terrestrial insects will also attack aquatic plants, particularly the marginal or bog plants. Grasshoppers frequently attack water iris, sweet flag (*Acorus* sp.), and cattails (*Typha* sp.). Crickets, scale insects, and weevils will also feed upon the pond's plants. Gall gnats (*Cecidomyiidae* sp.) will feed from inside wart-like protuberances. Gall attacks are easily remedied

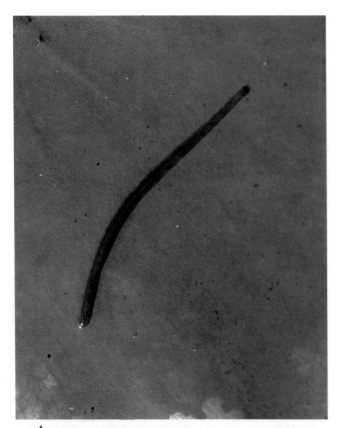

A common detritus-feeding leech may enter the pond on new plants.

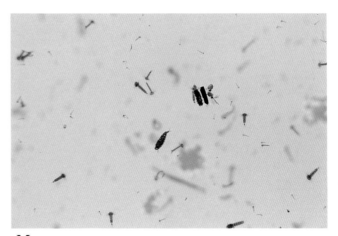

Mosquitoes lay their eggs in rafts. The young go through their larval stages before emerging from the water as adults.

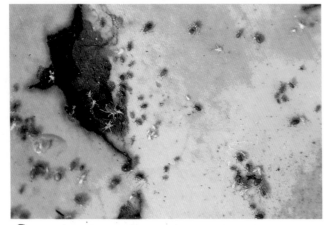

Several species of aphids will be drawn to weakened plants in the pond.

Non-aquatic caterpillars will invade and feast upon marginal plants.

*F*ishing spiders may be seen scurrying about the
pond's surface and on lily leaves.

*T*he three snails most likely to be encountered in the
pond are the Great Pond snail, the Ramshorn, and
the Trapdoor.

CLAMS OR MUSSELS

Introducing freshwater clams or mussels into the pool requires a media in which the crustaceans may travel and survive. Trays of sand or fine aquarium gravel will not cloud the water. Freshwater clams act as filters by drawing as much as a gallon of water every two hours through their shells as they feed upon free-floating algae and other minute organic particles. They should not be introduced into the pond until it is well established, lest the clams starve.

The swan mussel (*Anadonta cygnea*) is the species most frequently available from aquatic suppliers and pet stores. They may also be purchased from local markets. Be certain that such mussels are alive and are freshwater species. Dead mussels or saltwater species that quickly die in freshwater will pollute the pool with an incredible stench remedied only by a complete draining and cleaning. Often dead mussels will float. While freshwater clams may be found along creek beds and slow-moving streams, it is not advisable to bring them in from the wild as they may harbor parasites.

SNAILS

The Ramshorn snail (*Planorbis corneus*) and the Trapdoor snail (*Viviparis malleatus*) are generally considered beneficial to the pool. As scavengers, they aid with cleaning algae, decaying organic matter, and excess fish food from the pool. Because there have been reports of their damaging aquatic plants, and they have been observed in an aquarium quite happily consuming lettuce, they should be monitored for possible damage. The recommended stocking rate is one snail per square foot of pool surface.

The common pond snail, known as the Great Pond Snail (*Limnaea stagnalis*), will literally devour aquatic plants. It usually enters the pool on aquatic plants brought there. A program of disinfection of all new plants will usually negate the problem.

Floating cabbage leaves, lettuce leaves, raw chicken, or Styrofoam sheets in the pool overnight will attract those that may be present for easy removal. Since this snail can fertilize its own eggs, only one is required to start a problem.

Both the Ramshorn and the Great Pond snails lay their eggs on the undersides of lily leaves, as well as on other submerged vegetation. The Ramshorn eggs will be in a rounded, flat mass of jelly, while the Great Pond Snail eggs will be in an elongated string of jelly. A regular maintenance program of wiping the leaves with a soft cloth will dislodge the eggs. To prevent any opportunity of the Great Pond Snail eggs hatching, use paper napkins to wipe off the eggs and then dispose of the napkins.

The Trapdoor snail is a live-bearer. Its progeny are usually controlled by fish and insect predators. Excess Ramshorn and Trapdoor snails can usually be shared with other water gardeners or a local pet store.

In colder regions, snails will bury themselves in the mud of plant pots or on the pool bottom during the winter. They will usually survive if they are below any ice formed on the pool.

Apple Snails (*Ampula*), an unusually large tropical snail,will lay their eggs in rosy masses about the stems of aerial foliage. In temperate climates, they should be wintered indoors in an aquarium.

EXTERMINATING SNAILS

Because snails may be the host of many parasites and diseases, the pond-owner may decide to clear the pond of them. Netting them out or setting baited traps may not be completely satisfactory. A one-time dose of 2.25 mg/l of Chevreul's Salt ($CuSO_3 \cdot CuSO_3 \cdot 2H_2O$)

will be effective and safe for goldfish and koi. Cuprous oxide or copper protoxide (Cu_2O) at a dosage of 5–50 ppm may also be used. Dosages near 50 ppm may kill fish fry. Remove dead snails to prevent their decomposition from polluting the water.

The tropical apple snail (Ampula) *lays its eggs on aerial foliage rising from the pond.*

chapter eleven

PESTS

Mallard ducks, a common sight in even urban areas, will visit the backyard pond to feed upon tender submerged aquatics.

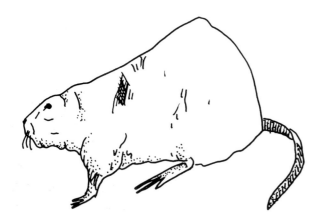

The muskrat and water rat are attracted to the pool by cattail and arrowhead plants. In the winter, voles may attack the pots, seeking the plant roots.

BEAVERS, MUSKRATS, AND VOLES

Beavers, muskrats, and voles will seldom visit the backyard water garden. Beavers and muskrats are more likely to be a nuisance in larger, earth-bottom ponds. While government conservation officers may assist in trapping beavers for relocation, the pond-owner is usually left to his own resources in dealing with water rats. Since the pests are most concerned with the tasty growth of reeds and grasses, it may be necessary to limit the number of such plants used in the pool. Animal traps are available from larger pet shops. Fencing the pool area may prevent some pests from accessing the pool; however, the fence should be of a solid or close-meshed type. Fine metal meshing that extends down into the soil will be of benefit.

OPOSSUMS

Opossums (*Didelphis* and *Phalangeridae*) may be "mystery" guests during the night hours in Australia, the United States, and now in Canada, where they have been introduced. The nocturnal feeders raid the pond and devour all surface plants with the exception of salvinia. Trapping the animals and releasing them in a distant area is a humane remedy.

Canadian water gardeners report the opossum as a night ravager of floating aquatic plants.

Raccoons will wade into shallow water in their quest for fish.

RACCOONS

Especially in the United States, raccoons, even in urban areas, present a problem as they raid the pond for tasty fish. Expert fishermen, raccoons will relish even the pond's largest fish. Shallow plant shelves provide the animal with handy access to their prey. Densely planting these areas with tall marginal aquatics will discourage some access, as will taller plantings around the pond's perimeter at these points. Water lilies placed near the favored fishing sites will give fish extra cover. Humane traps are available from pet supply stores or animal-control authorities.

TURTLES

Turtles can be a charming and entertaining addition to the pool. However, depending on the species, they will consume fish and/or aquatic plants. Vegetarian species feast on water lily buds and leaves. They should be captured, which may be no easy task, and relocated. Baby turtles can be captured by locating trays of dense submerged plants such as elodea in shallow areas of the pool.

Snapping turtles (*Chelydridae* and *Macrochelys*) that wander into the larger pool will remain as long as there are fish to eat. They can be caught by filling a plastic milk container half-full of water and affixing a large fish hook into the mouth of the container. The hook is baited with chicken liver, and the container suspended upside down in the pool with the bait submerged. Be very cautious in handling the hooked snapping turtle as they are aptly named. Calling on wildlife authorities may be a more practical option.

CRAYFISH

Crayfish (*Cambarus* and *Astacus*) are water crustaceans that wander into the pond from nearby streams and earth-bottom ponds. The larger ones will nip at fish. Even the smallest crayfish will totally consume submerged aquatics. A secretive pest, their presence may be discovered only by their shed skins. All plants may have to be removed from the pond in order to capture the crayfish.

Turtles, such as this painted turtle, although reputed to be vegetarian, are nonetheless known to eat small fish.

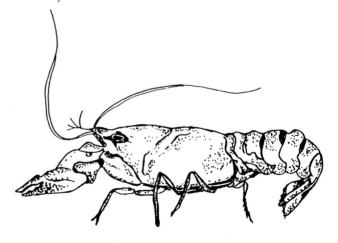

The secretive crayfish (*Cambarus*) may wander into the pool and greedily devour tender submerged plants.

A bullfrog floats motionless in the water awaiting the approach of an insect or small fish.

Toads may lay thousands of eggs that hatch into swarming masses of tadpoles seeking warm, shallow waters in late spring.

FROGS AND TOADS

Even the non-aquatic toads will visit the pool for breeding in the spring and early summer. Baby frogs and toads are known collectively as tadpoles. Generally a desirable pond inhabitant for their algae-eating habits, too many tadpoles may overload the pond's capacity. They are easily scooped from the pond on warm, sunny days when they mass together in shallow water.

Adult toads are beneficial to the garden for their aid in controlling insects. Adult frogs, however, especially the bullfrog, can quickly consume an entire fish population. If these visitors are undesirable, they may be controlled in several ways. Toads are easily captured from the garden. Frogs can be netted, but not without effort. It may be necessary to remove the plants to facilitate capture. Otherwise, after dark they are blinded by a bright flashlight and are easily captured. Even so, if a frog has discovered the pool, it is likely that others from whatever nearby water source will do the same.

If frogs are heard croaking or calling to each other, the pool should be carefully investigated for the translucent egg jelly that is laid among the plants. Frog eggs are laid in a mass of jelly; toad eggs are laid in long strands. To control the amphibian population, the eggs should be removed immediately as they will hatch in but a few days.

DUCKS AND GEESE

Although geese may visit only the larger of backyard pools, the mallard will visit even the smallest of pools. Being vegetarians, they will feast on the submerged aquatic plants at the pond's bottom. Besides feeding on some aquatic plants, they can ravage lily leaves and may bring parasites into the pool. They may also bring in a stray fish as well. If a bluegill appears mysteriously in the pool, he is probably a present from a visiting duck. Allowing the ducks to visit the pool may necessitate replenishing the pool's supply of submerged aquatics, as well as extra monitoring of fish for signs of parasites.

Another problem associated with allowing ducks and geese to visit the pool is excrement. Large masses of smelly algae may result, as might green water algae. Additional aeration and seed bacteria may be required to contend with the additional bio-load created by the visitors.

Ducks and geese may be steered clear of the pool by a human's or a dog's presence. Moving a scarecrow around the pond's perimeter may also frighten the ducks away. Suspending several aluminum pie pans near the pool may be effective, as may banging on a pan or firing an air pistol. Covering the pool with screening while the pool is unattended will prevent their access.

In the United States special care should be taken in warding off Canada geese as they are a protected species.

HERONS

Herons are unlikely predators in dense urban neighborhoods; however, they may prove to be quite pesky in less populated areas. The Great Blue Heron is the most familiar bird of the family, but other members such as the Green Heron or the American bittern may also visit the pool for dinner. They will feed upon the pond's fish both day and night.

The most commonly used remedy is to set out a heron statue near the pool. Reputed to be a lone feeder, herons may avoid the already occupied pool. Moving the statue every few days will help.

Covering the pool with screening or netting is the surest way of preventing a heron access to the pool.

*T*he Great Blue Heron can quickly consume the fish population of a backyard pond.

*T*adpole and Lilypad, two Jack Russell terriers known as "The Heron Patrol," are effective heron deterrents at Reimer Waterscapes nursery in Canada.

Likewise, creating a string network above the pool will also discourage it. Fish hatcheries have been known to erect wooden lattices above their ponds. Such a drastic measure, however, would not be easily tolerated by sun-loving aquatic plants.

Herons will avoid the pool if a human or an active

dog is present. Some dogs, such as the notorious Jack Russells of Reimer Waterscapes in Canada, can be trained to chase away herons. A lifelike scarecrow moved about regularly may convince herons a human is present. In practice, herons quite quickly learn the scarecrow is not a human.

Playing a radio outside by the pond may discourage a heron if the station selected is primarily conversation. An air pistol fired into the air on occasion can prove disconcerting enough to eventually convince herons to visit more peaceful feeding grounds. Live munitions should not be used since the heron is a protected species.

Since the Great Blue Heron is reputed to walk to the pool, some success has been reported with a fence of six inches in height strung with clear fishing line. Supposedly, the bird's legs touch the fence, and the bird then believes access is not available. However, herons have been observed to land directly in shallow water.

It may be that Indiana herons are particularly intelligent and fearless, but they have been noted to visit in groups of three, peer through windows, smile at the household, and indulge in fishing expeditions in the same pond as three or four golden retrievers. These herons seem swayed only by the most irate and animated of humans.

THE KINGFISHER

The kingfisher is another fish predator unlikely to feed in dense urban areas. It usually establishes an agenda and will visit a pond at the same time each day. This predictability makes it easier to anticipate the hours at which he must be discouraged.

Because his manner of fishing involves perching in a tree or tall shrub, if you keep the pool area free of such amenities, you will discourage his visits.

The usual methods of screening the pool or supplying a mobile scarecrow may discourage the kingfisher, as will the sound of a barking dog or an air pistol. A persistent fellow, he will remain in the area and return several times to see if the offending noise or presence has left.

NEWTS

Newts are secretive water salamanders that actually perform good deeds in the pool by helping to control insects. They are a bit slimy to touch and may provide a startle if encountered by accident. The only damage they might do in a pond is assist in the food chain with the disappearance of fish fry. Plants may have to be removed from the pool to net them out successfully, if desired. Generally, however, the usual pool will not be visited by them and will actually have to deliberately stock them.

The Eastern newt *(Notophthalmus viridescens)*, known as the red-spotted newt in its aquatic adult stage, feeds primarily upon insects, but will eat small fish and frogs as well.

SNAKES

Unless the pool is located near a larger body of water or a stream, true aquatic snakes are unlikely to appear in the backyard pond. Unless you are sure the snake is not venomous, it should be left alone and animal-control professionals called in to trap it. Caution

The common garter snake (Thamnophis) *may visit the pool for a tasty meal or two.*

CATS

The neighborhood cat can be a fish predator or tormentor. If the pond's water level is kept six inches below the extended stone edges of the pond, the cat will find it difficult to reach the fish. Shallow ponds that cannot accommodate a lowered water level should have dense plantings in the area of the cat's access. Pet stores offer products with an undesirable odor that discourage the presence of cats.

DOGS

Some dogs, especially the hunting breeds, enjoy the water. They will knock loose rocks into the pond or puncture holes in the liner with their toenails. Fish are traumatized and plants destroyed. The family dog should be trained not to play in the pond. Electronic collars are available from pet suppliers, if necessary.

If the dog-offender belongs elsewhere in the neighborhood, it is only polite first to contact the owner and request that the roaming pet be confined to a leash or fenced yard. In cases of non-cooperation, local animal-control authorities may need to be called. The pond area may need to be appropriately fenced.

should always be used in trapping a large snake since even non-venomous snakes can inflict painful bites when cornered. Venomous snakes have a distinctive triangularly shaped head. A non-poisonous snake may be a desired addition to a school science laboratory; possibly a local science teacher will be willing to trap the snake and remove it.

Garter snakes, however, may commonly pass through. A persistent harassment will usually convince the shy fellow that anyplace else is more desirable. Generally, they do not stay long, because most species are not true aquatic snakes. They will, however, partake of the fish during their brief sojourn.

CROCODILES AND ALLIGATORS

Depending on geographical location, crocodiles or alligators may be an indigenous reptile species that may stray into pools located near their habitats. Local authorities or animal control should be called for assistance.

*H*annah of Heidi's Haven is a diligent fish-stalker.

chapter twelve

CLEANING AND MAINTENANCE

*A maintenance program of good pool hygiene
ensures a successful, enjoyable water garden.*

CLEANING THE POND

If the pond is regularly kept free of debris accumulations, a thorough draining and cleaning will not be required more often than once every four to six years. Before starting the pool-cleaning, check with the municipal water supplier for the levels of additives.

Remove all plants. Submerged plants and water lilies should be placed temporarily in tubs of water. If they will be out of the pond for only a short time, they may be covered with wet newspapers or soaked burlap, enclosed in plastic bags, and placed in a shady area. Marginal plants may simply be set out of the pool. However, if roots are escaping the pots, they should be placed in water deep enough to cover them.

Remove fish to temporary quarters. It is best that such quarters be supplied with water from the pool itself. Aged and dechlorinated water may also be used. Provide aeration with an air pump and airstone or diffuser bar. If it is necessary to keep the fish in the holding facility for more than twenty-four hours, a nylon or mesh bag of zeolite should be placed in the tank to adsorb ammonia. Stress may be alleviated with the use of a stress coat and/or one or two tablespoons of salt per 5 gallons. Keep a bucket of pool water handy as the pool is drained for any fish that might be discovered hiding in the last waters of the pool's bottom. Feed fish daily when held in temporary quarters.

Drain the pool with the sump pump or a pool vacuum. Do not leave the pump unattended. The last remaining waters may be soaked up with towels and these wrung out into a bucket. If the pool is lined with gravel, stir the gravel as the pool is drained to remove organic matter. If the pool bottom is planted with submerged plants, an aquarium vacuum is the best method of draining and cleaning the gravel. The intake of the vacuum should be pushed straight down into the gravel and gently pulled up. The gravel will settle back

A pond with poor water quality and poor hygiene will have many problems, ranging from insect infestations to sick fish.

down onto the pool bottom while the sediment is pulled up into the hose. This procedure is followed methodically about the pool, taking care not to sever the roots of plants.

Scrub the pool sides with a stiff brush and hose down as the water level lowers. Check for any damage that might need repair. Refill the pool and treat for chlorine and chloramines, if necessary. Plants and fish should not be returned for at least two hours following treatment for chlorine. If there is a difference in water temperature between the freshly filled pond and the fish's holding facilities, place the fish in plastic bags of water and float them in the pool until the temperatures are equalized.

SPRING MAINTENANCE

Check the pool carefully for any areas that might require repairs. Conduct a partial water change of up to thirty percent. Dechlorinate as necessary. If possible, the water change should be conducted through the use of a pool vacuum. Set up the bio-filter after the water change has been dechlorinated and the water temperature has stabilized above 50°F. Feed fish sparingly only when they show signs of actively searching for food. Feed wheat germ type foods and avoid those with powder content that will add to the pond's bio-load.

Avoid changing pool water if an algae bloom occurs. Move any submerged aquatics and water lilies closer to the water's surface until the algae bloom has abated or plant growth merits a deeper placement in the pool. If treating an algae bloom with chemicals, follow dosage directions and remove dying algae to prevent feeding a recurrence. Since algicides will also slow other plants' growth, it is advisable to treat chemically for algae in conjunction with the first partial water change of the season. A half dosage of the algicide may then suffice. Remove any filamentous algae by hand or use an appropriate commercial treatment.

If the pool bottom is layered with gravel, pull any excess roots that may be scrambling about, especially those of invasive plants such as water clover. Allowing but one or two starts of such plants will prove more

*P*lants weakened by insect infestations, such as this "Pink Sensation," will attract aphids.

than sufficient for the season.

Provide aeration or spouting ornaments to prevent pockets of still water in the pool. Repot and divide plants. If the plants are not repotted, begin regular monthly feeding. Treat the pool with a broad-spectrum parasiticide to prevent fish infestations.

Provide temporary shade or shelter for fish until plant growth has resumed. An empty plant pot may be weighted with a stone to serve this purpose.

SUMMER MAINTENANCE

Keep dying leaves and spent flowers removed. Skim off pollens and seeds to prevent random germination in the pots of marginal plants. Water plantain (*Alisma*) and spike rush (*Eleocharis*) are particularly notorious for self-propagation throughout the pool.

Planting and division of plants may continue through mid-summer. Submerged plants may be propagated by cuttings or division. Thin out submerged plants such as elodea if they are choking water lilies or reaching the pond's surface and limiting the fish's swimming area. Thin and control invasive plants such as water clover (*Marsilea*) and floating heart (*Nymphoides*).

Net out insect pests such as whirligig and diving beetles. Watch for aphid, leaf miner, and moth attacks. Use a soft cloth to gently wipe stems and undersides of lily leaves every 7 to 10 days. If possible, remove and destroy eggs rubbed from the leaves.

Follow the five-minute feeding rule for fish to avoid adding to the pool's bio-load. Monitor fish population that may be increased by spawning. Many fry will be consumed by larger fish and predators such as frogs and dragonfly larvae. If it is desired to save the tiny fish, they should be netted and moved to an aquarium or a separate pool.

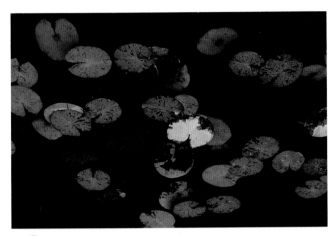

Dying leaves should be kept trimmed from the plants to prevent their decomposition in the pond.

Umbrella palms (Cyperus sp.) in temperate climates should be brought indoors before the first frost induces them into dying.

AUTUMN MAINTENANCE

Keep fallen leaves and debris from the pool. Leaves will settle to the pool bottom in only a few days and start decomposing. Many types of leaves, such as maple (*Acer*) and pines, will produce tannic acid that turns the water brown and can be toxic to fish. Netting or flexible fiberglass screening can be placed over the pool. Bridal-veil tulle is fine enough to trap pine needles, but should be handled carefully to prevent tearing. Netting may be unrolled from 2 × 4 lumber strips that will also help to anchor the screening.

Continue feeding fish what they will eat in five minutes. Switch to wheat germ type foods as the weather cools and their metabolism slows. If the water temperature goes below 50°F, stop feeding altogether. Do not resume feeding at all until the water temperature has returned to a consistent 50 to 55°F in the spring.

Stop feeding plants. Trim back the tops of marginal plants to prevent decomposition in the pool water and over-wintering of pests. Hollow stemmed marginals should be cut a bit above the water level to prevent rotting.

Prune all remaining water lily growth a bit above the plants' crown and lower the plants to the deepest part of the pool where they will remain ice-free. Other tender plants such as parrot's feather (*Myriophyllum*) and some varieties of pickerel (*Pontederia*) and arrowhead (*Sagittaria*) should also be lowered to a point where they will remain ice-free. Trim back submerged plants to below anticipated ice level to prevent freezing and resulting decomposition.

Prior to the first frost, tender and tropical marginal aquatics should be moved indoors and provided with a dish of water and strong light. Tropical water lilies should be removed and discarded or proper storage procedures effected. Tropical floating plants such as water hyacinth and water lettuce should also be removed and discarded. Although difficult to winter-over indoors, they may survive under strong grow-lights with a water temperature of 70°F.

If the pool is shallow and thick ice is probable, hardy water lilies should be removed in late autumn, cut

The shortening days of autumn often find water lily blossoms still open in the late afternoon.

back, and stored in a cool, but non-freezing area. Keep the plants moist by storing in plastic bags. Protect the bags with wire mesh if rodents may be present.

If a partial water change is conducted, it should be performed before the water temperature goes much below 50°F to keep from disturbing the fish.

If fish are to be wintered indoors, they should be moved by mid-autumn. The indoor tank should be set up with water from the pool. Fish should be watched for signs of parasites that tend to attack with temperature changes.

WINTER MAINTENANCE

If the pool will not freeze solid, raise the pump within a foot of the pool's surface to avoid recycling the warmer water at the pool bottom, where the fish winter. The waterfall may be run continuously on all but the coldest days to maintain an open hole in the ice. A tee may be attached to the pump and the pump moved to bubble just below the water's surface. If the waterfall tubing is not embedded in the pool's structure, it may also be accommodated to such a function.

If the pump is attached to a water fountain, remove the fountain head, cleaning and storing it in a warm, dry place over the winter. The pump itself may be used to keep an area of the pool ice-free.

Clean submerged mechanical filters and store in a dry location. They may be allowed to function through the winter if the pump is used as well. Drain bio-filters and clean media with a hose. Leave the drain valve or piping open to allow for water drainage and to prevent damage from freezing. The filter can be restarted in the spring once the water temperature has stabilized over 50°F. Sand filters should be backflushed and the valve or drain left open.

Keep the pool's surface from freezing solid in order to prevent the buildup of toxic gases that can kill fish:
• Use the pool's pump as previously described.
• Use a de-icer such as a pool heater, birdbath de-icer, or a stock tank heater usually available at farm implement stores.
• Float something that will prevent solid freezing, such as small rubber balls, plastic milk containers weighted with pea gravel, or sheets of Styrofoam. Black objects will absorb more heat. This remedy will help prevent ice-expansion damage to concrete and stone edgings.
• Cover the pool. See "Canadian Tips," pages 145–146.

If the pool should freeze solid, do not forcibly break a hole through the ice as the concussion may harm the fish. A pot of boiling water may be used to melt through the ice. If the ice is of any thickness, this process may involve considerable time.

Keeping the pump running just below the water's surface will keep a hole open in the ice over the winter.

CANADIAN TIPS

Heavy rainfall means contending with serious run-off and flooding problems. (See Chapter One, "Run-Off Contamination," pages 8–9, and "Rainfall Flooding," pages 9–10. Also, see Chapter Two, "Deteriorating Edges," pages 19–20.) In addition to these suggestions, Henry Reimer, of Reimer Waterscapes, recommends raising the pond edges four inches above ground level. This will be effective only if the liner is brought up behind the capstones. Reinforcing the pond perimeter soil with stiff concrete or a concrete collar will provide stability in saturated ground.

Heavy rainfall also portends the lush growth of weeds. Using landscaping fabric around the pond area and keeping the landscaping simple will enhance the enjoyment of the pond. The windward side of the pond should be planted with evergreen trees to act as a snow fence. This helps to ease the fury of "Alaskan" winds and allows the snow to remain as an insulating blanket on the pond.

Discarded water hyacinths make superb winter mulch for trees, shrubs, and the garden. The air-holding capacity of the plants provides insulation and the decomposing plants add valuable nitrogen and mineral nutrients to the soil.

It is important in the winter to keep at least a small hole free of ice to allow escape of methane and hydrogen sulfide gases. Should the pond freeze over, a cordless drill can be used to make a hole in the ice. Threading an airstone affixed to the tubing of a standard aquarium pump will help keep the hole open. The pump should be protected inside a ventilated, waterproof box.

Raising the pump to bubble just beneath the surface keeps an area ice-free and prevents disruption of the lower water where the fish are resting. If appropriate precautions are taken, there is no need to winter fish indoors, even though the pond may be but 2 feet deep.

Covering the pond with plywood boards is an old method that still works to insulate the pond. Aged plywood should be used to prevent unwanted pollutants from leeching into the pool. Plastic bags of leaves are stacked on the boards and then covered with a weighted tarp. The tarp prevents UV damage to the bags and preserves them intact for easy spring removal.

Harvey Macklin, of The Water Garden Network, suggests a plastic tent be erected over the pond. Construct a wooden base of 2 × 4's around the pond's perimeter. If heavy snows are likely or the pond is more than three feet wide, bolt cross-boards over the pond at three- to four-foot spacings. Center vertical boards may also be required for support. Boards, ½-inch piping, or rebar is used to form the side supports. They should be securely connected at the top with tee connections, clamps, or strong wiring to a horizontal frame. Drape heavy-gauge clear plastic over the form and secure this around the bottom with solid weights. Two layers of plastic create an insulating air pocket that can be filled with air mechanically, if desired.

A simple sawhorse-type construction insulates and protects lilies and fish during the cold winter months.

Major snow accumulations should be swept from the structure; light accumulations will add extra insulation.

WINTERING A HARDY WATER LILY OUTSIDE THE POND

The potted lily is removed from the pool, trimmed back, and placed inside a plastic bag to prevent its drying out. Store the bag in a cool, non-freezing location. Protect the bag with wire mesh if rodents might be present.

The lily may be removed from its pot and the soil thoroughly hosed from its tuber. After the leaves and roots have been trimmed from the tuber, the tuber is placed in a perforated plastic bag. Be sure to include the plant's label inside the bag. Submerge the bagged lily in non-freezing water of a temperature below 55°F. Change the water weekly to prevent rotting or souring of the tuber. Divide and repot in the spring.

WINTERING A TROPICAL WATER LILY

The successful over-wintering of tropical water lilies is not reliably consistent. For that reason, most sources recommend treating them as annual plants and discarding them at the end of the season. However, it is not impossible to over-winter these plants.

An easy method of wintering tropical lilies is to remove the lily from its pot and hose the tuber free of all soil. Cut off all leaves and excess roots. Cover the tuber in a pot of pea gravel and return the pot to the pool bottom where it will remain free of freezing. In the spring, the small tubers that formed at the base of the main crown can be repotted and set in the pool once the water temperature has warmed to 70°F.

Another method of variable success is to place the clean and trimmed tubers in airtight plastic bags of damp, but not wet, sand. If the sand is too wet, the tubers will rot. If the sand is allowed to dry out, the tubers will die. The bagged tubers may be stored in the vegetable bin of the refrigerator, where they will remain cool enough to satisfy dormancy requirements yet still avoid fatal freezing. Ed Graves, of Bloomington, Indiana, reports successful wintering of tropicals by storing the potted lilies intact within plastic bags in a dark place indoors. Simply repot and return them to the pond in the warming spring.

If the pool can be heated to a constant 55–60°F, the tropical lilies may be left in the pool. Cover the pool with a plastic tent to prevent frost damage to the leaves. Lilies maintained under these conditions will stop blooming and experience a partial or full dormancy, depending upon variety. If foliage remains on the plant, it will usually be reduced in size. The lilies should not be fertilized during this period. Pool heaters have too low a turn-on point for the successful wintering of tropical lilies in the pool. Such heaters are used only for maintaining a small area free of ice.

WINTERING OTHER TROPICAL PLANTS IN TEMPERATE CLIMATES

Tropical or marginally hardy reeds and grasses can be wintered indoors as houseplants. They should be set in dishes of water near a window providing bright sunlight. A grow-light may prove beneficial if the available sunlight is inadequate. These plants should be brought indoors before the first frost. Plants that have been subjected to but one hard frost may simply shut down and die.

Charles B. Thomas, of Lilypons, suggests how to winter tropical bulbous-type plants: Remove the plant from the pool before the first frost. Cut back the foliage and remove most of the soil. Place the plant in a cool, dry jar and cover the bulb with wet newspapers or a damp cloth. After two weeks, remove the plant and thoroughly clean the bulb. Store it in water for two weeks. Then pack it in damp, but not wet, sand inside a glass jar. Seal and label the jar and store it at 60°F for the winter. In early March, remove the jar's lid and fill the jar two-thirds with water. Place the jar

in a sunny window to sprout the bulb. Once the temperature outside has stabilized at 70°F, the plant may be repotted and returned to the pool.

The tropical umbrella palm (*Cyperus*) and papyrus may be overwintered by a method of propagation. Cut off the heads of the plants with a bit of stem attached and float them in water indoors under bright light. The heads will quickly root and may then be potted and treated as a houseplant for the remainder of the season.

WINTERING TROPICAL PLANTS IN WARM CLIMATES

All plants may safely remain in the pool in climates where the water temperature does not go below 60°F. True perennial plants that require a dormancy period will experience at least a period of slow growth, if not a brief dormant period. Plants that do experience dormancy should be cut back and allowed to rest in the pool. Do not fertilize the plants during this period. Resume feeding and repot, if necessary, once growth has resumed in earnest.

Covering the pool with clear plastic on cooler nights may result in tropical water lilies remaining in bloom year-round. So long as they are blooming, they should be fed monthly. If bloom ceases and the leaves display smaller growth, allow the plant to rest. Resume feeding only when the weather has become consistently warm.

During a period of cooler nights, heating the pool to a consistent 72°F will help maintain healthy growth. Tropical plants that actually experience dormancy will regrow from the roots and tubers when the weather warms.

Tropical plants such as water poppies may have to be grown in temperate zones as annuals.

APPENDIX ONE

THE JOY OF COLLECTING—
THE MICHAEL F. DUFF COLLECTION

N. Tetragona, day two

Odorata minor, day one

It is impossible for the water gardener to escape the mystique and fascination of the water lily. The photographs included here are a rare glimpse into one hobbyist's private collection that extends far beyond the offerings in popular catalogs to encompass delightful, sometimes forgotten, corners of the water lily world.

I. SPECIES

Species water lilies are genetically stable strains that have evolved naturally in nature. Species lilies are produced true by seed. These are but a few of the species naturally occurring in nature.

N. 'Alba' var. minor

II. MARLIACEA

This group of water lilies was hybridized by the renowned Bory Latour Marliac in the late 1800s. Considering this group his finest hybridizing achievement, Marliac gave them his own name. Of the group, 'M. Flammea' is a very rare cultivar and 'M. Ignea' is not commonly recognized.

Laydekeri 'Lilacea,' day two

'M. Flammea,' *day three or four*

Laydekeri 'Fulgens,' day four

III. LAYDEKERI

The laydekeri water lilies were hybridized by Marliac and named in honor of his son-in-law, Maurice Laydeker. These are an adaptable group of lilies, doing well in even half-barrel gardens. Of the group, laydekeri 'Rosea' is becoming very rare. Any of these varieties are difficult to purchase by mid-season as their smaller habits make them ideal specimens for the smaller pond.

'M. Ignea'

IV. MINIATURES

Pygmy and miniature lilies are especially suited to small ponds and tub gardens. Other miniatures are 'Graciella,' 'Indiana,' 'Chrysantha,' 'Paul Hariot,' 'Fulva,' 'Phoebus,' *N. pyg.* 'Helvola' and *N. pyg.* 'Joanne Pring.'

'Solfatare'

N. pygmaea 'Deva,' *day two and four*

'Comanche,' *day three and four*

V. SUNSETS, OR CHANGEABLES

These Sunsets, commonly sold as "changeables," are a unique group of water lilies that offer distinctive changes in color each day of their bloom. Other lilies offer but a fading or intensification of color. Sunsets can provide a delightful variety to the pond too small to accommodate several lilies.

N. pygmaea 'Rubra'

VI. RARITIES

Sometimes, lilies often mentioned in classic water lily literature are rarely seen today. For the most part, they are not widely cultivated, which can lead to their being "lost," as has been suggested of 'Goliath' and 'Graciella Alba.'

'Rosa Munda'

'Goliath,' *day two*

N. 'Graciella alba'

N. 'Deva,' *day 3*

VII. NEW HYBRIDS

New hybrids can occur naturally in nature by bee, insect, or wind cross-pollination. 'Peace,' 'Angélique,' 'Icicle,' and 'Albina' are naturally hybridized lilies discovered by Michael F. Duff and Craig Williamson in the ponds of Bee Fork Nursery in Missouri. 'Rosa Munda' is a new hybrid that was hand-pollinated by Reg and Clair Henley at Wychwood Carp Farm in England. '*N.* Deva,' its name meaning "Shining One" in Sanskrit, was hybridized by Michael F. Duff by crossing two different species of *N. tetragona*. It is the first true-white pygmy lily.

APPENDIX TWO

HELPFUL INFORMATION

COMPUTING POOL VOLUME IN GALLONS

1. Mathematical formulas
   a. If computed in inches, divide the total by 231.
   b. If computed in feet, multiply the total by 7.5.
   Rectangular shapes: length × width × depth.
   Circular shapes: 3.14 × radius^2 × depth.
2. Using a domestic water meter: Use a wrench to turn the locking nut on the meter to remove the lid. Record the reading before filling the pool. Subtract this figure from the figure recorded after filling is completed. No water at all should be used in the house during filling.
3. Using hose output: Fill a large bucket for exactly 60 seconds. Measure the water in pints and divide by 8 to compute U.S. gallons. Record start and stop times of filling the pool. Multiply the total minutes required for filling by the number of gallons the hose discharges in one minute.

COMPUTING POOL VOLUME IN LITERS

1. Multiply length × width × depth in meters × 28.41 for rectangular volume.
2. Multiply depth in meters × metric diameter^2 × 20.75 for circular volume.

COMPUTING SURFACE AREA OF POOL

1. Rectangular shape: Multiply length × width.

2. Circular shape: Multiply half the diameter by itself for the radius squared. Multiply that by 3.14.

FREQUENTLY USED EQUIVALENTS

ppm (parts per million) is equivalent to one milligram per liter of water

5 ml = 1 tsp.*
20 drops = 1 ml
60 drops = 1 tsp.
15 ml = 1 tbsp.*
2 tsp. = 1 dessert spoon
2 dessert spoons = 1 tbsp.
2 tbsp. = 1 fl. oz.
8 fl. oz. = 1 cup
1 cup = 48 tsp.
1 cup = 16 tbsp.
1 cup = 237 ml

*These figures are commonly supplied by most chart sources. However, using a standard, pharmacist-supplied, two-milliliter eye dropper and a standard kitchen measuring teaspoon, the equivalency was found to be 3 ml/tsp. and 9 ml/tbsp.

MATHEMATICS OF CONVERSIONS

To Convert	Multiply by	To Obtain
inches	2.54	centimeters
inches	25.4	millimeters

feet	30	centimeters
millimeters	0.04	inches
grams	0.035	ounces
ounces	28	grams
pounds	0.45	kilograms
milliliters	0.03	fluid ounces
liters	2.1	pints
liters	1.06	quarts
liters	0.26	U.S. gallons
fluid ounces	30	milliliters
U.S. gallons	3.8	liters

$= 1.8$ in.^{3}
$= 29.57$ cc
$= 29.57$ ml
$= 0.0296$ l

Celsius to Fahrenheit: Multiply by 9, divide by 5, add 32.

Fahrenheit to Celsius: Subtract 32, multiply by 5, divide by 9.

TABLE OF LIQUID EQUIVALENTS

1 milliliter (ml) $= 1$ cm^3
$= 1$ cc
$= 20$ drops
$= 0.20$ tsp.
$= 0.061$ in.^{3}
$= 0.001$ l
$= 1$ gm of water
$= 0.002$ lb. of water
$= 0.0003$ U.S. gal.

1 fluid ounce (oz.) $= 6$ tsp.
$= 2$ tbsp.
$= 0.0078$ U.S. gal.
$= 0.031$ qt.
$= 29.57$ gm
$= 0.062$ pt.
$= 0.065$ lb.
$= 1.04$ oz.

1 liter (l) $= 1000$ ml
$= 1000$ cm^3
$= 1.7598$ liquid pts.
$= 1.057$ liquid qts.
$= 0.264$ U.S. gal.
$= 203$ tsp.
$= 67.6$ tbsp.
$= 35.28$ oz.
$= 33.8$ fl. oz.
$= 4.23$ cups
$= 2.1134$ pt.
$= 2.205$ lb.
$= 61.025$ in.^{3}
$= 0.0353$ ft.^{3}
$= 1000$ gm
$= 1$ kg of water

1 U.S. gallon (gal.) $= 3.785$ l
$= 0.1339$ ft.^{3}
$= 231$ in.^{3}
$= 8.345$ lb. of water
$= 3785.4$ gm of water
$= 4$ qt.
$= 8$ pt.
$= 135.52$ oz.
$= 128$ fl. oz.
$= 3785.4$ ml

1 Imperial gallon $= 4.5459$ l
$= 0.1605$ ft.^{3}
$= 277.42$ in.^{3}
$= 4.845$ qt.

1 kiloliter (kl) = 1000 l
    = 264.18 gal.
    = 35.315 ft.^{3}

WEIGHT EQUIVALENTS

1 grain (gr.) = 64.8 mg
    = 0.065 gm
    = 0.35 oz.

1 gram (gm) = 15.432 gr.
    = 0.0353 oz.
    = 0.034 fl. oz.
    = 0.0022 lb.
    = 0.002 pt.
    = 0.001 l
    = 1000 mg
    = 0.001 kg

1 ounce (oz.) = 480 gr.
    = 28.35 gm
    = 0.0075 gal.
    = 0.03 qt.
    = 0.06 pt.
    = 0.0625 lb.
    = 0.96 fl. oz.

1 pound (lb.) = 5760 gr.
    = 373.24 gm

1 pound, avoirdupois = 7000 gr.
    = 453.6 gm
    = 16 oz.
    = 0.12 gal.
    = 0.016 ft.^{3} of water
    = 0.48 qt.
    = 0.96 pt.
    = 15.35 fl. oz.

    = 458.59 cc or cm^3
    = 453.59 ml
    = 453.59 gm
    = 0.454 l

LINEAR EQUIVALENTS

1 centimeter (cm) = 0.3937 in.
1 cubic centimeter (cm^3) = 0.0610 in.^{3}
1 cubic foot (ft.^{3}) = 7.481 gal.
    = 29.922 qt.
    = 59.844 pt.
    = 62.426 lb.
    = 998.816 oz.
    = 957.51 fl. oz.
    = 1728 in.^{3}
    = 28.32 l

1 cubic inch (in.^{3}) = 16.387 cc or cm^3
    = 0.0043 gal.
    = 0.017 qt.
    = 0.035 pt.
    = 0.036 lb.
    = 0.576 oz.
    = 0.554 fl. oz.

1 cubic meter (m^3) = 35.314 ft.^{3}
    = 61.024 in.^{3}
    = 1000 l

PARTS PER MILLION (ppm)

1 ppm = 1 mg/l
    = 3.8 mg/gal.
    = 2.7 lb./acre foot
    = 0.0038 gm/gal.
    = 0.0283 gm/ft.^{3}

$= 1$ oz./1000 ft.^{3}
$= 0.0000623$ lb./ft.^{3}
$= 0.0586$ gr./gal.
$= 8.34$ lb./million gal. water
$= 0.134$ oz./1000 gal.
$= 1$ oz./1000 ft.^{3} water
$= 1$ gm/264 gal. water
$= 1$ gm/m^3 water

1 gr./gal. $= 19.12$ ppm

PERCENTAGE SOLUTIONS

1 percent solution $= 38$ gm/gal.
$= 1.3$ oz./gal.
$= 10$ gm/1000 ml
$= 10$ ml/1000 ml
$= 10$ ml/l
$= 38$ ml/gal.
$= 1$ gm/100 ml
$= 1$ oz./0.75 U.S. gal.
$= 4.53$ gm/lb.
$= 0.624$ lb./ft.^{3}

COMPUTING SIZE OF PUMP NEEDED FOR WATERFALL

1. Fill a one-gallon bucket with water.
2. Time the number of seconds required to empty the bucket for the desired flow over the waterfall.
3. Divide 60 by the number of seconds for the gallons per minute and then multiply by 60 for the number of gallons per hour (GPH) required to produce the desired flow.
4. Measure the height of the waterfall from the location of the pump in the pool. Round up to the nearest whole foot. Add an additional foot for every 10 feet of hosing that will be required to reach top of waterfall. This is the lift required of the pump.
5. Find the lift in feet on the chart below and follow down that column to match with the desired GPH. If the required GPH is not listed, select the pump at the next-highest GPH. Since most water gardening pumps are sized by the GPH at one foot of lift, the one-foot lift column will be the size of the pump. Larger sump pumps are sized by horsepower ratings.

LIFTS	1'	3'	5'	10'	15'	20'
	120	70				
	170	140	100			
GHP	205	168	120			
	300	255	205	70		
	325	300	270	130		
	500	435	337	210	65	
	600	580	517	414	230	90
	710	690	670	580	380	150
	810	790	745	613	415	173
	1200	1170	1100	1000	840	520
1/6 HP				900	690	480
0.3 HP				2750	1750	750
0.4 HP				3250	2500	1550

RECOMMENDED TUBING BORE FOR PUMPS TO WATERFALLS

½ inch diameter	for flows up to	120 GPH
¾ inch diameter	for flows up to	350 GPH
1 inch diameter	for flows up to	1000 GPH
1¼ inch diameter	for flows up to	1500 GPH
1½ inch diameter	for flows up to	3000 GPH

If the length of the tubing is longer than 10 to 15 feet, the next-larger size tubing should be used.

ACKNOWLEDGMENTS

This book would not have been possible without the generous sharing of information by many special and knowledgeable people: James Allison; Dr. Gary Aukes of The Fishy Farmacy; Norman Bennett of Bennetts Water Gardens, in England; Kelly Billing of Maryland Aquatics Nursery; Ofer Borovsky of Mag Noy Israel Ornamental Fish, at Ma'agan Michael, Israel; Dr. J. N. Carrington of Interpet, Ltd., in England; Ray Davies of Stapeley Water Gardens, in England, and Latour-Marliac, in France; Joe B. Dekker of The Waterscaping Company; Bill and Lynn Dowden of Coastal Pond Supply; Michael F. Duff; M. Farmer of Stapeley Water Gardens, in England; Bob Friedman of Enviro-Reps International; Ben and Debbie Gibson of Perry's Water Gardens; Ed Graves of Ed Graves Landscaping; Eu It Hai of Oriental Aquarium (Singapore) Private, Ltd.; Clair Henley of Wychwood Carp Farm, in England; Harry Hooper of Mill Lane Nursery and Water Gardens, in England; Rob Huntley of the Aquatic Conservation Network, in Canada; Jim Hutson of Westfield Lighting; W. Clyde Ikins of Lakeside Gardens; Angelika Kern of Seerosen Kern, in Austria; Dr. Joe Kursch of Butler University; Jim Lawrie of Waterford Gardens; James Layton of Aquarium Pharmaceuticals; Randy LeFever of Blue Ridge Fish Hatcheries; Dan Lunsford of Custom Fountains; Harvey and Lois Macklin of the Water Garden Network, in Canada; Sarah Maurice of Mag Noy Israel Ornamental Fish, at Hazorea, Israel; Dr. W. Patrick McCafferty of Purdue University; John and Mary Mirgon; Dave Nash; Burt Nichols of Water Garden Gems, Inc.; Walter Pagels; Ben Plonski of Laguna Koi Ponds; Henry and Carole Reimer of Reimer Waterscapes, in Canada; Nick Romanowski of Dragonfly Aquatics, in Australia; Richard Schuck of Maryland Aquatic Nursery; Eberhard Schuster; Hideo Shimuzu of the Atagawa Alligator and Tropical Garden, in Japan; Perry D. Slocum; Peter Slocum of Slocum Water Gardens; Dave Smith of Serenity Ponds and Streams; C. B.

Stansfield of the British ADAS; Dr. Kirk Strawn; Philip Swindells; Charles B. Thomas of Lilypons; Dr. Jack and Nancy Todd, of Ocean Arks International; Joe Tomocik of the Denver Botanical Gardens; Karl Wachter of Wachter Stavdengärtnerei, in Germany; the staff of Sycamore Shoppe for Pets in Zionsville; the information researchers at the Indianapolis Public Library; and Brad Basey of Custom Computer Concepts.

The kind support and encouragement of the following are also much appreciated: Allgood Outdoors; Anglo Aquarium Plant Company, Ltd., in England; The Aquatic Habitat, in England; Bee Fork Water Gardens; Cherryhill Aquatics, Inc.; Cornish Aquatic Nurseries, in England; Earth Ponds Company; Hecht Rubber Corporation; Hillier Water Gardens, in Canada; Jungle Laboratories Corporation; Kester's Wild Game Food Nurseries, Inc.; Kordon, a division of Novalek, Inc.; Little Giant Pump Company; Lotus Water Garden Products, Ltd., in England; the Ministry of Agriculture, Fisheries and Food, in Great Britain; Moore Water Gardens, in Canada; Paradise Water Gardens; Patio Garden Ponds; Pondo-Mondo, a division of NU-LYFE Systems, Inc.; Potomac Waterworks; Reef Industries, Inc.; Resource Conservation Technology, Inc.; Scherer & Sons; Seepage Control, Inc.; Shady Lakes Water Lily Gardens; Sparsholt College Hampshire, in England; William Tricker, Inc.; Trident Water Garden Products, Ltd. in England; Van Ness Water Gardens; and the Waterworks/Tilley's Nursery.

A special note of appreciation goes to my editor, Hannah Steinmetz, whose intelligence, wit, and talent made the finer points of production an enjoyable task. Also, I am indebted to Ezra Steinmetz and Arie Levite for visiting Mag Noy Israel Ornamental Fish at Ma'agan Michael, Israel, to photograph their incredible koi and to Ruth Streett for making the initial contact with Mag Noy.

INDEX

PHOTO CREDITS

All photographs are by Ronald E. Everhart except as noted here.
Atagawa Tropical and Alligator Gardens, 74, 75, 96; Blue Ridge Fish Hatchery, 100, 115; Michael F. Duff, title page, 3 *(bottom)*, 6, 66 *(top)*, 99, 106 *(top)*, 148–151; Harry Hooper, 77; Arie Levite, 103, 104; John Mirgon, 3 *(top)*; Henry and Carol Reimer, 137 *(left)*; Nick Romanowski, 101; Bob Romar/Maryland Aquatic Nursery, 25 *(right)*, 33

Thanks to the following people in Indiana for graciously allowing their ponds to be photographed: Andre and Mary Arceneaux, Indianapolis (pond designed by Lance Hatieli), pages 29, 113; Hassel DePree, Bloomington (pond designed by Ed Graves), pages 16, 19, 27; Tom and Kathy Fixmer, Bloomington, pages 7, 9, 11 *(bottom right)*; Mr. and Mrs. George Grace, Anderson (pond designed by Custom Fountains), pages 14 *(top)*, 36; Ed Graves, Bloomington, pages 13, 14 *(bottom)*, 15, 26, 28, 44; Steve and Pauline Haley, Cicero, pages 8, 23 *(bottom)*, 24; Seymour and Pat Hoffman, Indianapolis (pond designed by Don Kelly), page 30; John and Martha Miller, Noblesville, pages 11 *(top)*, 12 *(top left)*; Shirley Rumple, Bloomington (pond designed by Ed Graves), pages 17, 25 *(top left)*; Dr. and Mrs. Larry Steele, Bloomington (pond designed by Ed Graves), page 97; Dan Walters, Carmel, page 54.

The line drawing on page 37 is from Maryland Aquatic Nursery. All other line drawings are adapted by Helen Nash, with assistance as follows: Page 8, from a drawing by Ed Graves; pages 63 and 74, from drawings by Lilypons Water Gardens; pages 127, 128, 129, from drawings in *Aquatic Entomology*, by Dr. Patrick McCafferty and Arwin V. Provonsha, Jones and Bartlett Publishers, Boston and London; page 10, from a drawing by Reef Industries; pages 15, 16, 18, 19, and 46, from drawings by Stapeley Water Gardens.